WINGED LEGEND

The Story of Amelia Earhart

WINGED

The Story of Amelia Earhart

LEGEND

by JOHN BURKE

G. P. Putnam's Sons
New York

Contents

Illustrations appear after page 128.

WINGED LEGEND

The Story of Amelia Earhart

1
Quality Hill

*I*T has been one-third of a century since Amelia Earhart and her navigator disappeared on a flight from New Guinea to Howland Island in the central Pacific. She has long since passed into the realm of legend as the most daring of the pioneer women aviators: the tousled, tomboyish young woman whom the newspapers celebrated as "Lady Lindy" and nominated as the feminine counterpart of Charles A. Lindbergh.

When she and her companion vanished over the Pacific on the next-to-last stage of their pioneering flight around the world, she was already one of the most famous women on earth. The manner of her presumed death and the impenetrable mystery which still surrounds it, which has not at all been dispelled by a curious reticence on the part of the American security agencies, has only increased her fascination. The legend will not die, nor will her spirit be laid to rest, until that mystery is solved.

Thirty-three years after her disappearance and presumed death it may matter little just how she died, whether in the crash of her plane or at the hands of the Japanese military who may have captured her and her companion on a forbidden overflight of the then-Japanese-mandated Micronesian islands. It is the thirty-nine years of her life, not the moments of her death, that count with posterity. It is the answer to the question, What impelled a small-town Kansas girl, later a Boston social worker, to risk her life time after time? Why did she volunteer for the select company of Everest climbers, polar explorers, astronauts, desert wanderers, and others obsessed by the urge to hazard their lives on going where no other humans have ventured before? The motivations of that rare breed, growing rarer in a computerized and more circumscribed world, are still one of the great mysteries of the human spirit; and if we could grasp its meaning, we would learn much more about why and how our species differs significantly from other forms of animal life.

Certainly there is more to human adventure than the it-was-there-so-I-had-to-climb-it cliché, or the obligation felt to expand the frontiers of humanity, or even the curiosity some have declared to be divine. It seems to be part of the same compulsion that persuaded the evolving species to venture out of the mother sea, to come down out of the trees while lesser primates gibbered at the foolhardiness of it all, and later to leave the safety of their caves. Something drives humanity on toward a goal it cannot visualize, and certain individuals feel that impulse more strongly than others.

A few days after Amelia Earhart and Fred Noonan disappeared and hope for their recovery was abandoned, Walter Lippmann commented on her career with a compassionate wisdom that makes his words as poignantly true today as they were thirty-three years ago. In his newspaper column he wrote that he could not quite remember the stated purpose of Miss Earhart's last flight, but it was the spirit that animated the venture that counted for more than any practical results in the development of aviation.

"The best things of mankind," he wrote, "are as useless as Amelia Earhart's adventure. They are things that are undertaken, not for some definite, measurable result, but because someone, not counting the costs or calculating the consequences, is moved by curiosity, the love of excellence, a point of honor, the compulsion to invent, or to make or to understand. In such persons mankind overcomes the inertia which would keep it earthbound forever in its habitual ways. They have in them the free and useless energy with which alone men surpass themselves.

"Such energy cannot be planned and managed and made purposeful or weighed by the standards of utility or judged by its social consequences. It is wild and free. But all the heroes, the saints and the seers, the explorers and the creators, partake of it. They do not know what they discover. They can give no account in advance of where they are going, or explain completely where they have been. They are possessed for a time with the extraordinary passion which is unintelligible in ordinary terms.

"No preconceived theory fits them. No material purpose actuates them. They do the useless, brave, noble, the divinely foolish and the very wisest things that are done by men. And what they may prove to themselves and to others is that man is no mere creature of his habits, no mere automaton in his routine, no mere cog in the collective machine, but that in the dust of which he is made there is also fire, lighted now and then by great winds from the sky."

Certainly "no preconceived theory" encompassed the character and personality of Amelia Earhart, no matter what her public image. If many adventurers are somewhat harebrained and feckless, she was cautious and longheaded about confronting danger, a mistress of the calculated risk. The adventurer as a type is not long on intellect, but Amelia Earhart was a literate and highly intelligent woman. There was no harum-scarum element in her disposition; she was brought up to be a lady and lived up to her upbringing.

The short, tousled hairdo, the exuberant all-out grin that lit up her face when photographers set off their flashguns, the slacks and leather jackets she wore around hangars and airdromes all suggested the grown-up tomboy, but she was exceedingly feminine and wrote poetry on the sly.

The public saw her as a happy-go-lucky young woman blessed with an optimism that allowed her to overlook the hazards of her later career, but she had suffered her share of psychic wounds. Publicity pictured her as the barefoot girl from Kansas, a sort of female Tom Sawyer, who presumably tinkered with the insides of old automobiles as soon as she was old enough to lift a monkey wrench, as she wryly acknowledged in one of her memoirs. "Whenever anyone asks me about my work in aviation, I know that sooner or later I shall hear, 'And, of course, you were mechanical when you were a girl, weren't you?' As a matter of fact, in a small way, I was—witness the trap I made to catch the chickens that strayed into our yard."

The scenario of her childhood, however, could have been written by Eugene O'Neill in one of his darker moods. She was born just after the frontier had been smoothed down and all the trail-town gunfighters had been laid to rest in their Boot Hills, after the sod-busting pioneers had finished their labors, after the Plains Indians had been driven off the Kansas steppe and into reservations; but the "stockade mentality" still existed. So did the sociology of the raw new frontier towns: the displacement of the adventurers, the pioneers, the groundbreakers as the elite by the bankers, town promoters, and businessmen. That displacement made for social and political conflict between the conservatism of the new establishment and the pitchfork-waving Populism of the sodbusters who figured that somehow they had been cheated and downgraded.

Both elements were present in Amelia Earhart's background, and indirectly their inability to fuse, to accommodate each other, was responsible for a family tragedy—banal in some of its aspects to anyone with insight into the often balky workings of American democracy and its inequities, but no less real and painful to those who experience them.

The trouble was that her maternal grandparents lived on Quality Hill in Atchison, Kansas, and saw their daughter as a belle of the rudimentary prairie society, while her father came from a hardscrabble farm on the other side of the Atchison, Topeka & Santa Fe tracks.

Her mother's side of the family, the Otises, were quality folk by Kansas standards. Her maternal grandmother came of a Philadelphia Quaker family and journeyed as a bride to Kansas when it was untamed. "Great piles of buffalo bones lined the newly built railroad tracks when *she* came and Indians in blankets were always to be seen in the town," her granddaughter recalled. "I remember her telling me of their crowding about her when, as a young housewife, she went to market. They lifted the lid of her basket and peered within, and felt the fabric of her dress, until she was quite terrified, mistaking their native curiosity for some kind of sinister threats."

The man who had brought her out to the savage wilderness just before the Civil War was Alfred Otis, the stern embodiment of the Victorian male with his fixation on material success. He loomed over Amelia's childhood, over her father and mother and sister, like a thunderhead always menacingly poised on the horizon. Alfred Otis came of First Family stock and never forgot it. One of his ancestors was Gebhard Harres, a German-born industrialist. Another was James Otis, whose protest against the British writs of assistance was termed the first shot of the American Revolution. Alfred Otis himself took up the law as a member of the first graduating class of the University of Michigan.

Then, with his Philadelphia bride and his law books, he moved out West to help establish the rule of the law. He was one of a select company of energetic and able young men who decided to establish the town of Atchison, just north of Kansas City, on both sides of the Missouri River. A wise choice, it must have seemed, when the Santa Fe Railroad selected Atchison as the terminus of its line to the Pacific Coast.

Among Otis' collaborators in town-building were such men as Colonel John A. Martin, editor of the Atchison *Daily Champion* and later governor of Kansas; J. J. Ingalls, who was to be the U.S. senator from territorial Kansas for eighteen years; Albert Horton, a future judge of the Kansas Supreme Court; James Brewer, who became a justice of the United States Supreme Court—the lawyers and politicians were plentiful among Atchison's founders—Baily Waggoner, later a railroad magnate; and John Lippincott, later chancellor of the University of Kansas.

Otis and his friends were all Northerners and pro-Union men. During the days of the night riders (raiding across the border from the slave state of Missouri), the Jayhawkers, the barn-burners, and mounted guerrilla bands fighting mostly for loot, they lined up firmly on the Union side. The Southerners who had helped found Atchison and settle the countryside were encouraged to leave, no doubt with little gentleness.

When the Civil War broke out, they all joined the Kansas Volunteer regiment formed under the leadership of Colonel Martin. It was not one of the more distinguished regiments. It was sent to Mississippi early in the war and floundered around the swamps for several months before being sent back to guard the Kansas border. The rest of the war was spent quite comfortably in barracks at Fort Leavenworth.

During the postwar years Otis, like his johnny-come-early friends, prospered professionally and financially. He became judge of the United States District Court and adopted a suitably overbearing manner; if not the hanging-judge type, he certainly did not quail at sitting in judgment on other men. He also became the president of a bank and grew wealthy on land speculation. His home on the bluff overlooking the Missouri was among those of its peers, the solid men of Atchison. One of his wife's sisters married Dr. Paul Challis, who owned the showplace of Quality Hill; *his* brother, Luther Challis, the manager of the *Daily Champion,* had been a New York stockbroker and had brought the original charges against Victoria Woodhull and her sister, Tennessee Claflin, which drove those free-swinging feminists into exile. Judge Otis and his friends, including Colonel Martin and Senator Ingalls, believed in equal opportunity, of course, but only up to a point; for their own children—including Amelia Earhart's mother—they established the exclusive Latin School. His daughter, Amy, would have gone on to Vassar if she had not been stricken with diphtheria when she was sixteen.

One chronicler of those postwar years in Atchison, the most acerbic, was Ed Howe, the editor of the Atchison *Globe*, a sardonic and iconoclastic fellow who gained national renown as "The Sage of Potato Hill" and the author of *The Story of a Country Town*. He took over the editorship of the *Globe*, and assumed the role of prairie philosopher, in 1877. Atchison was then a town of 12,000 and "had many bright men," he observed in his autobiography; "most country towns are drained dry of their best men by the cities, but Atchison in the old days had aspirations and prospects. It had been the headquarters of the Ben Holliday stage line, and of freighting to the West: the early trails from California, Colorado and Montana led to Atchison, and many of the big buffalo and Indian tales were first told there. It had a railroad before Kansas City, and was an interesting, promising place with history and 'characters,' including a gang of the most noted three-monte men in the West."

To Howe, not given to giddy enthusiasms, "there was something about the land agents, the hotel keepers, the editors, the citizens, the farms, the houses, that was unforgettable. No writer has ever correctly described the West of that day; it cannot be done with ink and paper, or brush and canvas."

What he loved most of all about pioneering Atchison was not the bigwigs like Judge Otis and his friends on Quality Hill but the cheerfulness of its ordinary citizens, most of whom were desperately poor. "One man was so witty that I have always remembered him: and his wit was displayed in telling about the poverty of himself and neighbors. One of his exaggerations was that the people were so poor they had no postage stamps, so when they wanted to write back home, advising their friends to join them in what they called 'God's country,' they pinned a side of bacon to the letter, and it went through. This was possible, the wag said, because the hogs were so thin, owing to lack of food, that a side of bacon was no thicker than a postage stamp." Kansans of the sod-hut class endured dust storms so thick that farmers got lost in their own fields, blizzards that buried their homes to the rooftops, and Indian raids of the ultimate in ferocity. "The settlers lived from the sale of buffalo bones, everywhere bleaching on the prairies. . . . Their only fuel was buffalo chips [that is, dried buffalo manure] and occasionally they were the subjects of Aid campaigns, some of which later resulted in the rise and fall of statesmen."

From this beleaguered class, but without the sardonic humor recalled by Ed Howe, came the other side of Amelia Earhart's family. Her father was the youngest of twelve children born to what some people would call an "educated fool," a Lutheran minister-missionary sent to the Kansas frontier equipped to teach Greek and Hebrew but not to support a large family in any degree of comfort. The Lord, it was thought, would provide.

If the genes, the venturesome spirit that impelled Amelia Earhart to fly where no human had ever flown before, could have been isolated, they probably owed more to that luckless paternal grandfather of hers than to the pompous and consequential Judge Alfred Otis. The Reverend David Earhart was descended from Hessians who migrated to Pennsylvania before the start of the American Revolution. Rev. Earhart was ordained an Evangelical Lutheran minister, married, and brought his family to Kansas in 1860, about the same time the Otises arrived. They never met socially. "This part of the country was newly settled and was mostly settled by poor people," David Earhart wrote in a pamphlet describing his family's history and published in 1898, the year of his famous granddaughter's birth, "and had had three years of hazardous border warfare and two successive years of grasshopper depredation.

"It was difficult to fix people's minds upon godly living when they were sore put to find food sufficient to sustain life. By teaching school and other secular labors, I managed to live and rear my family, though often put to great straits. Often johnny-cake and turnips provided our main meal."

On Sundays the Reverend Earhart rode 50 miles on horse-back to serve his scattered congregations. Weekdays he taught Hebrew and Greek at Midland College, a small Lutheran school on the outskirts of Atchison, and worked his small dust-blown farm nearby.

In his brief memoir Rev. Earhart recalled an incident involving Amelia's father, Edwin, then seven years old, that illustrated the family's struggle against their hostile environment. He returned home late one Sunday afternoon from his pastoral circuit-riding to find that Edwin had broken the Sabbath by going fishing and "had caught six large and succulent bull-heads. I immediately asked him how it happened that he had desecrated the Lord's Day by fishing. He replied, 'Sir, you know fish always bite better when you are preaching.' I reproved him for his levity, but, to tell the truth, I found it hard to refrain from smiling at his ingenuous excuse."

A family council was summoned to decide whether, given the lack of any other form of protein in the larder, to eat the fish or keep the Fourth Commandment. It must have been a difficult decision, with all those hollow-eyed children waiting to be sustained either by fried fish or Christian orthodoxy. The issue was decided in the true spirit of Hessian practicality, which the British army had once found such a vexing matter. Mrs. Earhart suggested, "Husband, let us consider Edwin's fishing a work of necessity which is permitted by Holy Writ, for I think the children need nourishment. You and I will abstain, but it seems wrong to refuse the gifts of nature because of the day." Rev. Earhart allowed himself to be persuaded. "What could I say? Truly there is no answer to an upright woman's plea for her children's welfare; so the fish were cooked, and, as there were ample for all, both his mother and I partook of Edwin's catch, although I must admit my conscience was not entirely clear."

Despite his youngest son's "levity," Rev. Earhart was determined that Edwin also take up the ministry. Edwin was dispatched to a theological school in Pennsylvania and was graduated with scholastic, if not spiritual, honors. "Greatly to my disappointment," his father recorded, "he declared he did not feel the call to the ministry, but professed a leaning toward the law." Young Edwin had only to lift his eyes to the big houses on Quality Hill to learn the difference between a lawyer's prospects and a preacher's.

Edwin Earhart, a lean, dark-haired, handsome young man, worked his way through the University of Kansas law school by shining shoes, tending furnaces, and tutoring his less brilliant but better-heeled classmates. It might have been the beginning of a Horatio Alger story, except that there were certain flaws in Edwin Earhart's character, certain amiable weaknesses, that would be magnified with the years. He had a winning way, an ability to charm (suggested by the Sabbath-breaking incident) that often goes with an aversion for facing hard realities.

While Edwin Earhart was working his way through law school, Amy Otis, living in another world on Quality Hill, was learning to be a lady of high expectations. She and Constance Ingalls, the senator's daughter, were the leaders of Atchison's junior-division society. "There were military balls at Fort Leavenworth and cotillions at St. Joseph, where the young people went up river by a specially chartered steamer," one of her two daughters, Mrs. Muriel Earhart Morrissey, has written. "They returned by midnight and were met at the landing at the foot of Commercial Street by the sleepy drivers of the family carriages to be carried up the steep road to the pleasant homes on the Hill." Amy also became an accomplished horsewoman and, as her father's evident favorite, "enjoyed listening to and participating in the discussions of public affairs which took place when Senator Ingalls and former Governor Martin gathered on the wide hospitable verandah of my grandfather's home."

Obviously Judge Otis hoped and planned for a brilliant marriage for his daughter: marriage to a man of substance, not some young striver hopeful of making a place for himself. Even in the early nineties it was apparent to pragmatic men like Judge Otis that young people without a head start on their fellows could waste the best part of their lives struggling for a foothold. That, he swore, was not for his Amy. To train her for her role as the wife of a man of affairs he often took her with him on trips to Utah and the Indian Territory when he went to inspect land offered as security for loans from his bank.

His ambitions for his daughter were quenched, ironically, the very night Amy Otis made her formal debut in Atchison society at what was then called a presentation ball. The ball was held in the garden of the Otis home under the firefly glow of Japanese lanterns. An orchestra from St. Joseph played waltzes, the Lancers, the Virginia Reel. Judge Otis, beaming on the elect of Atchison society, wondered which of the more promising sprigs of local aristocracy might marry his pretty and carefully raised daughter.

Unfortunately for Judge Otis' hopes, his son, Mark, had brought home a classmate from the University of Kansas law school. Mark Otis introduced the guest to his sister: "Amy, this is Edwin Earhart, the law student who has pulled me through this year's examinations."

Years later Amy Otis would tell her daughters, "I liked him right away and I soon knew that he liked me."

That mutual attraction did not extend to Judge Otis. He could not visualize an impoverished minister's son as his son-in-law. The fact that Earhart was also a lawyer did not help his case. Where were the influence, the money, the connections a man needed as much as his certificate from the bar examiners? Sizing up young Earhart from the eminence of a judge's bench, but with unjudicial prejudice, the resentful father may also have found fault with Edwin's easygoing nature, his amiability, his winning manner—not at all the qualities of a great advocate. He might have forgiven the impoverished background if Earhart had exhibited the drive, the ruthless ambition which might make up for that handicap. Nor was he moved in the slightest by the romantic fact that his daughter and Edwin Earhart had fallen in love at first sight.

Judge Otis, in his heavy-handed way, aimed to make it as difficult as possible for Edwin and Amy to marry. An extended delay, with other more promising men strewn in her path, might result in a change in Amy's heart. But Amy was single-minded, and Edwin Earhart could not be persuaded that he was unworthy of the daughter of Judge Alfred Otis. His own family could boast of a great-uncle, Private John Earhart, who had been killed in action during the American Revolution. And if the Earharts had not prospered as greatly as the Otises, his father could still write that "there was not a drunkard among the whole number of our kin. Nor do I know of any bearing our name to have been arrested for crimes of any kind."

Finally Judge Otis told young Earhart that he could marry Amy, but only on the condition that he prove himself financially capable.

"I expect any gentleman who marries my daughter," Otis declared, "to be able to show an income of at least fifty dollars a month, with the prospect of increasing as time goes on."

Edwin Earhart, attorney at law, sweated it out. Most of the legal business around Atchison was sewed up by old established firms. It took him five years, in fact, before he could prove to Judge Otis that he had brought his income above the required minimum. The judge did not join in the young couple's elation.

A small quiet wedding took place at Trinity Church on October 18, 1895. There was no honeymoon. Edwin Earhart and his bride simply traveled by train to Kansas City, Kansas, where Judge Otis had provided them with a completely furnished home. That wedding gift in itself was a vote of no-confidence in the bridegroom, suggesting that Earhart on his own would never be able to provide a decent home for his family.

During the next several years, as her daughter Mrs. Muriel Earhart Morrissey makes plain, there was a painful "period of adjustment" for the young bride. "The transition from pampered debutante to poor man's wife was made with some tears and some unhappy hours. . . ."

Their first daughter, Amelia Mary, named for her two grandmothers, was born July 24, 1898; their second daughter, Muriel, three years later. For the birth of her first child Mrs. Earhart was persuaded to come home to Atchison. Then and later she and her daughters spent much time at her parents' home while Edwin Earhart was absent from Kansas City settling claims for the railroads; it was steady work, and he wasn't aggressive enough, perhaps, to compete with other lawyers for the larger fees. Judge Otis was not at all reluctant to assume the role of surrogate father in addition to grandfatherhood.

His suspicions of Edwin Earhart's competence as a breadwinner were unabated—and in that disgruntlement lay the makings of tragedy for his son-in-law, his daughter, and their children. The judge's attitude was justified by events, but a wiser and kindlier man would have concealed it. Earhart was a dreamer, a rainbow-chaser, and his habit of imagining himself an overnight millionaire was not eradicated by family responsibilities.

Instead of hunting down possible clients, just after his two daughters were born and his domestic burden was increased, he occupied himself with an invention he was convinced would make his fortune. It was a device for holding the signal flags carried on the rear car of every train. After making models of his invention, he journeyed to Washington to secure a patent, full of hopes that he could sell the flag-holder to the Rock Island Railroad, which often employed him in claims-settlement work.

A letter to his wife from Washington told how the dream had fallen apart. The Patent Office informed him that another inventor had secured a patent on the same sort of device two years before. Undaunted, he refused to cry over "spilled milk or outdated patents," he wrote Mrs. Earhart. Characteristically, he sought refuge in his dreamy ambitions: "I must recount a feeling which I experienced as I walked past the glorious buildings which house our lawmakers and the great legal minds of the Supreme Court. I felt that I shall some day mount those marble steps in an official capacity. . . . Who knows?"

His brief enthusiasm for invention had even more disastrous consequences than the wasted trip to Washington. Several months after his return, a city tax collector appeared at the Earhart home. He informed Mrs. Earhart that the year's tax had not been paid. Mrs. Earhart insisted that he was wrong, that she had saved $41 for the payment and given it to her husband.

When Earhart returned home that evening, he had to make a confession. "Amy, the collector was right. I used the tax money toward getting my patent. I was so sure I could easily pay it when I got the money for the idea [his signal-flag holder] from the railroad." *

To obtain the delinquent tax money, Earhart sold a collection of law books which Judge Otis had given him. More embarrassment. One of the lawyers to whom Earhart had sold three of the books later mentioned the transaction to Judge Otis. The latter was outraged, demanded an explanation, was even more outraged by the explanation, and castigated his son-in-law with the direst accusation in any respectable Victorian's vocabulary—"poor provider."

Grandpa Otis' anathema seemed quite justified to him the following year. Earhart received a $100 windfall for settling a railroad right-of-way dispute, and instead of sensibly depositing it in Grandpa Otis' bank, he took his wife, six-year-old Amelia, and three-year-old Muriel off to see the St. Louis World's Fair and blew the hundred dollars on riotous sight-seeing and roller-coaster rides.

* Recounted by Mrs. Muriel Earhart Morrissey in her candid and enlightening memoir of her sister, *Courage Is the Price,* Wichita, 1963.

Looking back on their early childhood, his two daughters remembered it as a happy time. After the World's Fair trip, they built their own rickety roller coaster, enlisting the help of their young uncle, Carl Otis, and constructing a shaky trestle from the roof of their father's toolshed. The test pilot, naturally, was Amelia, who was growing up to be a towheaded tomboy. The little cart she occupied while it hurtled down the track ended up running off the trestle and dumping its passenger. Amelia dusted herself off after her first crash landing, and the girls' mother, attracted to the scene by the sounds of the small disaster and Muriel's wails, put an end to any further experiments with the roller coaster. About the same time, of course, a whole generation of pioneer fliers was endangering its young limbs by jumping off barn roofs with umbrella parachutes or building kites strong enough to bear a boy aloft; so Amelia Earhart was well within a tradition waiting to be born.

Amelia and Muriel spent more and more of their time at their maternal grandparents' big house in Atchison. As Amelia would recall, "I was named for my grandmother and was lent her for company during the winter months. I am sure I was a horrid little girl, and I do not see how she put up with me, even part time."

By "horrid" she meant that she was a tomboy who refused to behave in the demure style, all hair ribbons and starched dresses, ready to simper for the approval of the nearest adult. She and her sister attended a private school, the College Preparatory School, in Atchison. She was a bright pupil, but "I never qualified as teacher's pet."

Then and later, both as a tomboy and a budding feminist, she resented the fact that girls were not permitted to show much interest in athletics, were reminded by frowning elders that they should be content with their dolls and mock tea parties. Any hoydenish tendencies were quickly squelched.

Amelia looked back on those days when she was being trained to be a proper lady by her grandmother with a lingering resentment. "I know that I worried my grandmother considerably by running home from school and jumping over the fence which surrounded her house. 'You don't realize,' she said to me one day, 'that when I was a small girl I did nothing more strenuous than roll my hoop in the public square.' I felt extremely unladylike and went around by the gate for several days in succession. Probably if I'd been a boy, such a shortcut would have been entirely natural. I am not suggesting that girls jump out of their cribs and begin training, but only that the pleasure from exercise might be enhanced if they knew how to do correctly all the things they can do without injuring themselves or giving a shock to their elders. Of course, I admit some elders have to be shocked for everybody's good now and then."

Their parents, however, had more advanced views on bringing up the two girls. Mrs. Earhart's only sister, Margaret, was a follower of Amelia Jenks Bloomer, the Kansas suffragist, who advocated a new style of dress for females. To liberate them from skirts she devised "bloomers," also known as "gymnasium suits," which she adapted from the baggy Turkish pants (not, perhaps, realizing that they represented the ultimate in feminine subjugation, the Ottoman harem). At Aunt Margaret's suggestion, Amelia and Muriel were provided with bloomers. They were also subjected to a certain amount of ostracism from proper little girls in the neighborhood. According to Amelia's recollection, "though we felt terribly 'free and athletic,' we also felt somewhat as outcasts among the little girls who fluttered about us in their skirts. No one who wasn't style conscious twenty-five years ago can realize how doubtfully daring we were."

Undoubtedly Amelia, in particular, was set apart from the other girls on Quality Hill. One Christmastime she began a letter to her father, "Dear Dad: Muriel and I would like footballs this year, please. . . ." They received not only footballs, but Amelia (then about nine years old) was successful in wheedling a .22-caliber rifle from her father, which she and Muriel used for shooting rats in a nearby barn. The Earhart girls were also supplied with boys' sleds on which they could take belly whoppers instead of sedately riding upright as other little girls did.

Their father also took them on fishing trips as soon as they were old enough to cast a line, whenever he showed up at Grandpa Otis' house to enjoy a spell of the judge's dubious hospitality.

It was a happy, carefree girlhood, despite the long separations from their father and often their mother, who sometimes accompanied Earhart on his claim-settling trips. If there was constant money pressure in the Kansas City home, it still wasn't critical enough to concern the Earhart daughters. "Throughout the grade school period, which was mostly spent in Atchison, I remember having a very good time," Amelia later wrote. "There were regular games and school and mud-ball fights, picnics, and exploring raids up and down the bluffs of the Missouri River. The few sandstone caves in that part of the country added so much to our fervor that exploring became a rage."

The two girls inherited their mother's love of horses and riding, but their grandmother objected to Amelia and Muriel taking up the same sport. That didn't prevent Amelia from sneaking a ride occasionally on whatever horseflesh was available. Two girls she knew were the daughters of a butcher, who kept two elderly draft horses to haul his wagon. Amelia learned to ride on their backs when the horses weren't being used to make deliveries. One summer when their parents took the girls to a Minnesota lake on vacation, she came across an elderly but spry Indian pony. "He could be bribed by cookies to do almost anything. No saddle was available, so half the time my sister's and my riding consisted of walking back home."

The only pet in their lives was a large black mongrel they named James Ferocious, ordinarily an amiable beast who pulled the Earhart girls in a wagon and allowed them to decorate his shaggy frame with bits of ribbon. One day some boys invaded their backyard and began tormenting James Ferocious, who was tied up. The enraged dog broke his chain and tore after the boys, who escaped his slavering jaws only by jumping on the roof of a shed. The neighborhood was alerted by shouts of, "Mad dog." Amelia, as her sister recalls, calmly walked up to the quivering animal and talked to him in a normal tone until the boys could make their escape.

The greatest pleasure of her girlhood, Amelia recalled, was not her more harum-scarum adventures as the tomboy of Quality Hill but reading her way through her grandfather's library. By the time she was nine or ten she had read the works of Walter Scott, George Eliot, Charles Dickens, Victor Hugo, Alexandre Dumas, Oliver Optic's boys' books, and the heavy bound volumes of *Puck, Harper's Weekly, Youth's Companion,* and *Harper's Magazine for Young People.*

Amelia was irked by one thing about the children's books and stories she read—they were mostly written about and for boys. Years later she was still annoyed, in retrospect, by that tendency in children's fiction. In an unpublished essay on the subject of juvenile books, prepared for a librarians' meeting, she noted that "girls are not expected to join in the fun" of childhood adventure. "There are no heroines following the shining paths of romantic adventure, as do the heroes of boys' books. For instance, who ever heard of a girl—a pleasant one— shipping on an oil tanker, say, finding the crew about to mutiny and saving the captain's life (while quelling the mutiny) with a well-aimed disabling pistol shot at the leader of the gang! No, goings-on of this sort are left to the masculine characters, to be lived over joyously by the boy readers.

"Of course girls have been reading the so-called 'boys' books' ever since there were such. But consider what it means to do so. Instead of closing the covers with shining eyes and the happy thought, 'That might happen to me someday!' the girl, turning the final page, can only sigh regretfully, 'Oh, dear, that can never happen to me—because I'm not a boy!' "

Such reflections, recalled from girlhood, may well have shaped her determination to show the males of the species that she could equal if not outdo them. When she was a girl, of course, women could not vote and were otherwise deprived of their civil rights; any who stepped over the line carefully drawn by their menfolk and willingly—or not, in the case of feminists —observed by the women themselves, were regarded as freaks, deviants, mutants of some repulsive variety.

Amelia, however, believed (as she wrote in the essay quoted above) that there wasn't all that much difference between the sexes. "It has become pretty evident that the female of the species is not so radically different from the male in her reactions to life if her education is at all similar. Because this world has been arranged heretofore so that women could not be active as individuals, it has been assumed that they neither wanted to nor ever could be. However, so many 'impossibilities' have been proved baseless in the last quarter century that there is no telling now where limitations to feminine activities—if any— will be henceforth . . . if women are eventually found in loco-motive cabs, building bridges, or chasing bandits as normal occupations, it will be no surprise to me."

There is no doubt that even as a child of nine or ten Amelia stood out as markedly individual, not merely because of her boyish pursuits and her refusal to conform but because of her courage, determination, and curiosity. One of her Challis cousins, Lucy, who lived next door to the Otises, once was asked what made Amelia Earhart remarkable as a child. She replied that children didn't analyze each other, but "all I knew was that Amelia was more fun to play with than anyone else—I admired her ability, stood in awe of her information and intelligence, adored her imagination, and loved her for herself—and it held true always."

In 1907 the pattern of the Earhart girls' childhood—winters spent mostly in Atchison, the rest of the year in Kansas City— was broken when the first real opportunity presented itself in their father's life. For almost a dozen years he had been enduring a hand-to-mouth existence settling claims for the Rock Island and other railroads on a fee basis. Most of his work was for the Rock Island system, with its headquarters in Chicago.

The crispness and literacy of his reports of claims settled, occasionally enlivened with a touch of humor, appealed to the railroad's general counsel, George MacCaughan. The latter now proposed that Edwin Earhart join the Rock Island's claims department in Des Moines, Iowa, on a salaried basis. Earhart was elated; no more scrabbling for assignments, no more worrying over gas bills and grocers' accounts. He would be able to maintain his family in comfort, if not in style, and furthermore, he would be able to detach them all from the manorial influence of the Otises.

The girls, it was decided, would be left with their grandparents one more time while their father and mother looked for a suitable house in Des Moines. It was expected that the house-hunting would take two months at the most. Instead, it was almost a year before Mrs. Earhart, still influenced by the standards of Quality Hill, found a house in Des Moines which she considered suitable.

This was the last extended stay the girls would make with their aged grandparents, both of whom were rapidly failing in health. Judge Otis retained his juridical humor and his aristocratic sensibilities. Once, during their year's stay with their grandparents, Amelia and Muriel went exploring a fenced-off section of their grandfather's property; it was close to the crumbling bluff overlooking the Missouri, and the girls had been forbidden to venture there. They wriggled under the fence and to their great delight found an old outlaw's cave littered with whiskey flasks. Their story of the afternoon's adventure was received with shock and indignation by their grandmother, who reminded them that they had been warned away from that section of the property. "But you never told us not to squeeze under the fence," Amelia protested. "She's right," her grandfather ruled. "No *ex post facto* laws, according to the Constitution."

The girls were also impressed by their grandfather's hauteur when arc lighting was extended to Quality Hill. No arc light on the North Terrace, Grandpa Otis informed the city; the brilliant illumination would attract insects and make sitting on the veranda uncomfortable in the summertime. Work on the lighting system was suspended while Judge Otis negotiated with the authorities. He admitted that the city had a right to light the streets, but North Terrace would be illuminated according to his own specifications. At his own expense he had a gas lamp with a mellower glow set up in front of his property. One of his servants was detailed to light the gas lamp every night within seconds after the city's arc lights went on.

Watching Grandpa Otis' private street lamp being lit at dusk was the last memory the Earhart girls carried away with them of the home on Quality Hill, their grandparents, their childhood, and their last moments of absolute security.

2
"The Girl in Brown, Who Walks Alone"

AMELIA EARHART'S first glimpse of a genuine airplane, or "aeroplane" as it was then spelled, came one summer's day when her father took the family to the Iowa State Fair in Des Moines. Aviation then was in its first toddling stages, and the first aircraft were rickety affairs of wood and wire and oiled canvas, powered by tiny sputtering engines. "Flights" were a matter of a few miles, often terminated by engine failures and forced landings among the cornstalks.

Earhart watched impatiently while Amelia and Muriel indulged themselves in the childish pleasures, the merry-go-round and the pony rides and buying paper hats. He was eager for his first look at a plane; it had been only a few years since Wilbur and Orville Wright faltered into the sky over the sand dunes of Kitty Hawk.

Finally their father managed to round up his family and escort them over to the flying field on the edge of the fairgrounds. Amelia, though uninterested, would remember later her first sight of the machine which some twenty years later would make her a world celebrity, engage her whole life, and encompass her death. It was an unimpressive contraption, as she would recall: a biplane with the pilot, his face masked by goggles, sitting with his feet on the crossbars, the engine and a big wooden propeller behind him. The engine coughed. Ungainly as a gooney bird, the craft trundled along the rough surface of the pasture; its rusty ailerons creaked, and suddenly it floundered into the air.

Edwin Earhart was transfixed by the miracle of man-made flight and tried to interest his daughters in the spectacle. But Amelia could not be distracted from fussing with her paper hat and wondered aloud when they could return to the merry-go-round. So much for first impressions. . . .

Living in a city the year round, with no long stays with their grandparents (both of whom died while the Earharts were living in Des Moines), came as an unwelcome change for Amelia and her sister. They could no longer run tomboyishly wild in the semirural neighborhood of Quality Hill. And they saw little more of their father, since he often had to leave Des Moines on claim-settling junkets for the railroad. The only compensation was that he often took his family along in a private car provided by the Rock Island.

There was also the vexing matter of their schooling. There was no private school nearby. Public school was ruled out by their mother when a neighbor remarked that Amelia's blond braids would have to be cut off because every child attending that facility got head lice the first week in school and it was easier to eliminate the lice if the child's hair was short. Mrs. Earhart simply could not visualize the grandchildren of Judge Alfred Otis with lice-infested hair being doused with kerosene, nor their associating with children whose parents brought them up under such conditions.

For their first year in Des Moines the Earhart girls were taught by a private tutor paid twenty-five dollars a month, despite the strain on Edwin Earhart's resources. A year later, however, Mrs. Earhart decided that her daughters might profit more from being taught with other children. Amelia and

Muriel were sent to the nearest public school and did not pick up any lice, which apparently were only a rumor vigorously broadcast by people offended by the fact that Negro children attended the same school.

Amelia attended public school in Des Moines for the seventh and eighth grades, then the first years of high school. Those several years marked the end of whatever emotional security she had known in her childhood. In her memoir *The Fun of It*, those years and their psychic wounds were passed over in a few sentences; she skipped from Des Moines to her final high school years in Chicago with the remark that "I went to at least six high schools but managed to graduate in the usual four years' time. . . . I've never lived more than four years in any one place and always have to ask 'Which one?' when a stranger greets me by saying, 'I'm from your home town.' "

The trouble which broke the cocoon of security came from her father. Like many men, he could endure the chanciness of living from hand to mouth, because it engaged all his energies, but prosperity was ruinous. His father had boasted in the monograph which recited the Earhart family history that the clan had never produced a drunkard, but the Reverend Earhart had understandably failed to take into account the future behavior of his youngest son.

During their first year in Des Moines, everything seemed to be going smoothly for the Earhart family. As a reward for his diligence, Edwin Earhart was promoted to be head of the Rock Island's claims department and given a salary almost double the one he had been receiving. He was also provided with a private railway car for any trips he had to make. Subsequently the family moved to a larger house in a more attractive section of Des Moines, where, presumably, there were not even rumors of head lice among schoolchildren.

Then came the period of which Muriel Earhart would write, the "hardship and mental suffering" which "made an indelible impression on us and help to explain some of Amelia's actions and attitudes in her later life."

On the doorstep to middle age, Edwin Earhart had suddenly discovered the temporary and illusory joys of alcohol. Probably he had the alcoholic temperament, the fatal predisposition, all along. Daydreamers are generally hit the hardest. Furthermore, men who wait until late in life to tackle what was then euphemistically called John Barleycorn, often succumb the quickest, having never acquired the head for alcohol. One could almost hear Judge Otis groaning "I told you so" from his grave back in Atchison.

Suddenly and with shattering impact the melodrama of alcoholism intruded upon the lives of his wife and daughters. It has been described with candor and sympathy by his daughter Muriel in her memoir *Courage Is the Price*.

One Saturday afternoon the Earhart girls and a number of neighborhood friends eagerly awaited Earhart's return from the office. Every weekend he led them in a game of cowboys and Indians, himself assuming the role of Chief Geronimo with the boyish zest which was one of his most attractive traits. He even dressed in an Indian costume for the game. Afterward he and the children would sit on the steps of the Earhart home and be served cookies and lemonade by Mrs. Earhart.

This Saturday Earhart came home a little late. The children saw him get off the streetcar a block away and ran, whooping and shouting, to meet him. They were a little puzzled by the fact that his step was uncertain, his smile wobbly.

"Can't play today," he told the children. "Don't feel very good."

Mrs. Earhart was waiting at the door and started to tell him that his Geronimo costume was laid out and waiting for him, then her face froze. She helped her husband inside.

Next morning, pale and sickly, he drank black coffee for breakfast and ignored the usual popovers and scrambled eggs which their cook served on Sunday mornings. While the girls were changing into their churchgoing clothes, Mrs. Earhart slipped into their room and made a brave attempt at explanation. "You see," she said, "every once in a while some of the men in Dad's office ask him to drink with them, and he says he can't always refuse without seeming very rude. That's what happened yesterday. We must try to keep him from doing it again because it's bad for him and bad for his work for the railroad."

Mrs. Earhart had already been informed, but did not tell her daughters, that while intoxicated the previous day her husband had dictated several bellicose and indiscreet letters which his secretary had held up pending a sober second look.

Everything seemed all right that day. On the way home from church, Earhart put his arm around his wife's waist and assured her, "I guess if you and the girls will forgive me, God will, too, and I promise I'll walk the straight and narrow from now on."

He did not keep the pledge, however, and two or three times a week he came home lurching and thick-tongued. "Dad's sickness," it was referred to between Mrs. Earhart and her daughters. The rest of the story had all the banality—and painful truth—of a temperance film. Earhart's work began to suffer. Some of his reports to the main office in Chicago were inaccurate. As his behavior became more and more erratic, Mrs. Earhart and the girls, having no experience in dealing with a drinking man, greeted him coldly, scornfully, in a united feminine front. Perhaps nothing could have saved him, not the warmest sympathy and understanding, hard as they are to summon for the delinquent; but their method could only make things worse.

His daughters, at least, came to understand the root of his problem in later years when they gained more experience of the world. Edwin Earhart, it seemed to Muriel, had always unconsciously resented having to accept favors from the Otis family. Coming to Des Moines broke that bond of condescension, and "Dad was at least savoring one of the pleasures which poverty had denied him." His drinking companions, hardened topers who could hold their liquor, "applauded his opinions and made him feel he 'belonged' as he had never felt with Mother's relatives. . . . I can see the mistakes we made. . . . Our attempts to make him stop drinking only made his home uncomfortable and alien; it created a vicious circle."

One afternoon, just after a liquid lunch with the boys, he returned to his office to find a letter from his friend and sponsor, George MacCaughan, informing him that the railroad was becoming dissatisfied with the slipshod quality of his work and warning him to "stay away from that drinking crowd and do your work for the railroad in the creditable manner that you have done it, up until now."

Earhart had just enough drinks in him to scrawl a hot-tempered and insolent reply to MacCaughan.

On receiving it, MacCaughan caught the next train to Des Moines. He arrived at Earhart's office in the claims department about four in the afternoon. Earhart and another man, flushed and unsteady, were sinking a bottle of whiskey between them. MacCaughan grimly sent his protégé home in a cab, then called Mrs. Earhart and told her he'd be out later in the evening for a private talk about her husband's condition.

That night MacCaughan persuaded Mrs. Earhart that the only hope was to send her husband away for "the cure." In those days, that meant a local branch of the Keeley Institute, which specialized in treating dipsomania. The Keeley Cure, a nightmarish fragment of many a family legend in the pre-Prohibition years, administered a drug that was supposed to make a man or woman violently ill if he took another drink—at least until the drug wore off.

Earhart maintained that he could stop drinking any time he really wanted to but finally allowed himself to be committed to the Keeley Cure. "Once I get all cleaned up inside," he swore to MacCaughan and his wife, "I'll never touch another drop. God knows what liquor can do to a man. I promise I'll never try to be that kind of 'good fellow' again."

About a month later Earhart returned home clear-eyed and apparently "cured." Mrs. Earhart had installed a carpenter's bench in the basement in hope that her husband would occupy himself with a constructive hobby. His daughters had earned three dollars between them picking cherries for a neighbor and bought him a new fishing rod and reel. Earhart was brimming with optimism and expressed the opinion that when the Rock Island reinstated him his true worth would be appreciated and in a year or two he would take George MacCaughan's place as general counsel when MacCaughan retired.

He stayed sober for a time, while the drug he had been given wore off, and then began taking a few nips to while away the time until the Rock Island got around to reinstating him. About that time his mother-in-law died, leaving a will which Earhart regarded as a personal affront. Mrs. Otis left an estate of close to a million dollars which was to be divided among her surviving children, but her daughter Amy's share—alone of the bequests—was to be held in trust for twenty years . . . or until Edwin Earhart died. She had heard of his "sickness" and feared that if she left Amy's share to her outright, Earhart might lay hands on his wife's share of the fortune and drink it up. She wanted to be sure that her daughter had the trust income to fall back on, that her granddaughters would be properly educated.

Earhart seized upon the will as an excuse to step up his liquor intake. The Rock Island, learning that he had not conquered his problem with alcohol, refused to reinstate him. His home became a small hell as he alternately brooded and raged over the Otis will and the final "insult" it offered him.

He pulled himself together sufficiently to write letters of application to other railroads, but somehow they were all aware of the sorry circumstances under which he had left the Rock Island's employ. It was the spring of 1913 before he was finally offered a clerk's job in the freight office of the Great Northern Railway in St. Paul, Minnesota.

Prosperity may have started him on his drink career, but adversity did little to halt it. His salary barely covered the cost of the large house they rented in St. Paul; the family budget was sustained by income from Mrs. Earhart's trust. Amelia entered Central High as a junior and became fascinated with physics. It was difficult for her mother to adjust herself to "reduced circumstances," to the anomalous role of a freight clerk's wife. She had a wealthy and socially prominent uncle living in St. Paul whom she hoped would introduce her and her family to the local aristocracy. But the uncle and his wife paid one rather furtive duty call and were never seen or heard from again. Thus her hopes were dashed that Amelia and Muriel might be proposed for membership in the exclusive skating club and the predebutante cotillion assemblies.

In her midteens Amelia regarded herself as a rather plain, homely girl with her towhead, freckles, and lean, boyish figure. Though she grew up to be an exceedingly attractive woman, it was a conviction that never really left her. As a young girl, however, she maintained that it didn't really matter that she would never be the belle of the ball. "I don't think that boys particularly cared for me," she wrote, "but I can't remember being very sad about the situation. Probably I didn't get so much exercise at dancing as I should have liked, because of having only one or two faithful partners." Already she had decided that there would be more important things in her life than boys and parties. And even then, perhaps, she had formed the determination never to be dependent on any male. The example of her father, much as she loved him, would always be in the foreground of her mind. One remnant of her most impressionable years as the daughter of a drinking man was her refusal to touch anything alcoholic.

Her father continued his disastrous bouts with the bottle in St. Paul. One night he came rushing home, elated because he had been given a chance to return temporarily to claims settlement work. A Great Northern freight train had been wrecked near Albert Lea, Minnesota, and the claims department was shorthanded. Amelia was helping him pack when she found a bottle of whiskey stowed away in one of his suitcases. She uncorked it, took it over to the sink, and was pouring it down the drain when her father, blazing with anger, came into the kitchen. He approached the girl with his fist raised, but Mrs. Earhart caught his arm and he subsided in abject contrition.

Thanks to Amelia's intervention, he did well on that job. A few weeks later, however, he was assigned to another claim, got drunk while investigating it, and involved the Great Northern in a long hassle over the ensuing complications. After that he was kept inside at the freight office.

One social event to which the Earhart girls looked forward was the Twelfth Night party at St. Clement's Episcopal Church, which they attended. Two boys in particular had urged them to come to the dance. Whether they could depended on their father's sobriety. In those days it was the practice for well-bred young ladies to be escorted to such an affair by their fathers, who danced with them once, then left the party and returned to take them home before midnight.

On that evening Earhart had promised to be home early enough to have dinner, change clothes, and take them to the party at eight o'clock. Once again he let them down. He staggered home shortly before eight in no condition to perform his fatherly duties. Muriel rushed upstairs and wept, but Amelia, she recalled, "scorned to pound her pillow and cry . . . she went stoically into the living room."

The family's resources were strained several months later when Earhart lurched into the path of an automobile and had to be hospitalized briefly. Little wonder that his daughter Muriel included in her prayers a plea for the success of Carry Nation and her saloon-smashing campaign.

There was nothing carefree about the rest of Amelia Earhart's girlhood. Every evening she and her mother and sister would wait anxiously for her father's return, listening for his footsteps to determine whether or not he had been drinking. Nothing seemed to work out for the family. They packed up once more and left St. Paul when Earhart was promised a job in the claims department of the Burlington Road at Springfield, Missouri. It all turned out to be a misunderstanding. The employee whom Earhart was to replace had decided not to retire, after all. As compensation, he was given four weeks' work as a small-claims adjuster.

After that misfortune it became clear that Edwin Earhart could no longer be relied on as a breadwinner; the family would have become objects of public charity if it hadn't been for the income from Mrs. Earhart's trust fund. Earhart obviously needed time to win his own battle with his personal demons and get back on his feet. There seemed to be no alternative but to break up the family temporarily. The Shedd family, whom the Earharts had known in Des Moines, had moved to Chicago and invited Mrs. Earhart and her daughters to stay with them as long as they wanted. Meanwhile, Earhart would go back to Kansas City, live with his sister and her family, and open a law office.

Mrs. Earhart and the girls journeyed to Chicago and moved in with the Shedds in their Morgan Park home. Apparently the recent years of anxiety, shame, bewilderment, and sheer bad luck had not crushed Amelia's spirit. She was determined to get through school on schedule and find some way of helping her father. Quite possibly she felt more sympathy for him than for her mother; she could not despise him for being defeated by circumstances, even though many of them were self-engendered.

Even as a girl of seventeen she had the strength of character and the insight to realize that some people are better endowed to face reality than others. She would never allow herself to be hammered into the ground as her father had, or to be at the mercy of others' opinions and prejudices, but she could understand that there was more to the problem than dismissing him as an alcoholic weakling. A curious tolerance developed in the girl; instead of bitterness, she acquired compassion. Later in life two of the men to whom she entrusted her life as an aviator had problems with alcohol similar to her father's, but she would not discard them despite the risks involved—and that was a peculiar grace indeed for the daughter of an alcoholic to have acquired on her own.

Her pride and self-possession were obviously intact while she and her mother and sister were living on the bounty of the

Shedd family. Amelia was determined to get the best possible grounding in scientific subjects. The nearest high school was Morgan Park High, which her sister attended. Amelia, however, refused to enroll until she had inspected the chemistry laboratory. "It was just a kitchen sink," she declared, refusing to attend the school. She then interviewed the principals of several other high schools and found their facilities inadequate for her senior year, which might, for all she knew, be the end of her formal education. Finally she settled on Hyde Park High School because it offered adequate courses in chemistry and physics.

During her final year she became involved in a miniature student revolt which turned out to be a dud. The teacher of her English class was an elderly deaf woman who reportedly held onto her job because she was related to the mayor's wife. The teacher was utterly incompetent, and her classes were a shambles. Amelia tried to get up a petition for her removal, but those who signed it became frightened or were subjected to parental pressure and withdrew their signatures. Rather than stay in the riotous classroom and waste her time, Amelia demanded and received permission to spend the English period in the school library, where she read four times the number of required books for the course. The caption under her picture in the yearbook for the graduating class of 1916 was singularly apt: "The girl in brown, who walks alone."

She was also singularly lacking in what was then called "school spirit." When the graduating class marched up to the platform to receive their diplomas in June of 1916, Amelia was not among them; she simply had no further use for Hyde Park High School, and it was another sixteen years before Mayor Cermak of Chicago, somewhat to her surprise, pressed the diploma on her at a civic function in her honor.

3
Nursing the War Wounded

*T*HE summer of Amelia's graduation, she and her mother and sister moved back to Kansas City. Against considerable odds, it appeared that Edwin Earhart had found his footing. Alcohol was never a serious problem again, though by then the damage to his marriage, if not to his relations with his daughters, was probably irreparable. He was practicing law again, and that was all to the good. All his drinking had been done while working for someone else. Like some of the pioneer fliers Amelia was to know, Earhart evidently was braced, challenged, by a certain amount of insecurity.

He had found a small house, and the family was reconstituted. Another threat to the Earhart girls' future education, however, loomed. Mrs. Earhart learned that her brother, Mark Otis, had been unwise in acting as guardian of her trust fund from their grandparents' estate.

The $60,000 which Amy Earhart had received in trust had been sharply diminished through her brother's handling of the fund. He had sold some of the low-interest but "safe" bonds which had been handed down by their mother and invested the proceeds in the common stock of several enterprises which promised higher returns but went broke instead.

As a lawyer, as the husband of the legatee, and as the father of two girls depending on that trust fund for their higher education, Edwin Earhart was outraged. He urged his wife to ask the court to dissolve the trust and give her the principal in a lump sum. The trust had lost $15,000 in four years, he pointed out. But Mrs. Earhart was understandably reluctant to take her own brother into court, even more so to have family affairs made public. She finally yielded to her husband, and the plea to break her mother's will was heard in a courtroom with the portrait of her father staring down on the proceedings.

Mrs. Earhart's action was supported by her mother's doctor, who testified that Mrs. Otis was "unduly harassed by worry and illness" when she changed the will. The court then ordered the trust dissolved and the remaining principal turned over to the beneficiary.

Waiting for that issue to be settled, Amelia stayed out of school until funds were available for furthering her education. Then she entered the Ogontz School, a sort of girls' prep, now the Ogontz Campus of Pennsylvania State University. Later she planned to attend Bryn Mawr. But it soon developed that Amelia was not quite the Ivy League type.

Scholastically, she was more than a match for her surroundings. "Amelia," said Miss Abby Sutherland, the headmistress of the Ogontz School, "was always pushing into unknown seas in her reading. The look in her straightforward, eager eyes was most fascinating in those days. Her most characteristic charm was her poise, her reserve, her curiosity." In her late teens she was still coltish, not nearly so obsessed by her appearance or by her effect on boys as most of her contemporaries. Rather significantly, Miss Sutherland added that "she helped very much to impress the overindulged girls with the beauty and comfort of simple dressing."

Socially, she was still the nonconformist, the odd girl out. She was invited to join one of the three secret sororities and enjoyed being a member until she learned that some of the girls at the school were excluded from joining any of the secret societies. Her efforts to persuade her own sorority to take in more members, anyone who wanted to join, were met with failure, so she carried her case to the headmistress.

"Every girl," she told Miss Sutherland, "ought to have the fun of belonging to a sorority if she wants to."

That crusade failed, but she maintained a rebellious posture in other ways. Rabindranath Tagore, the Indian poet with a lushly romantic style, was the smash hit of the girls' school lecture circuit in those and succeeding years. He made an impressive appearance at Ogontz, where the girls read his poetry and feverishly discussed his mystic philosophy. One of Amelia's classmates expressed the hope that Tagore, a Hindu, would soon to be converted to Christianity.

"Why should he?" Amelia crisply inquired, shocking her classmates.

Some of the more ardent Christians on the campus thereupon accused her of being an atheist. Amelia insisted that she believed in God. She did not believe, however, in many of the things she had been taught in Sunday School. To her, she explained, God was "a power that helps me to be good." How a person worshiped Him, she added, was that person's own affair.

Most of her schoolmates came of upper-middle-class families and were largely preoccupied with hopes of making good marriages. But Amelia's mind evidently was focused on finding a career for herself; she pasted clippings in a notebook telling of the achievements of various women throughout the world who were taking over jobs previously reserved for men. She was not impressed, however, by legislation then being proposed to permit women to own property and maintained that "women will gain economic justice by proving themselves in all lines of endeavor. . . ."

For her Christmas vacation in 1917 she journeyed to Toronto to visit her sister, who was attending St. Margaret's College there. As a believer in direct action, she experienced another change of course during those dreary winter weeks. The World War was then entering its climactic phase, and the base hospitals of Toronto were jammed with casualties from the Western Front. "There for the first time," she later wrote, "I realized what the World War meant. Instead of new uniforms and brass bands, I saw the results of four years' desperate struggle; men without arms and legs, men who were paralyzed and men who were blind."

One day when she and Muriel were walking along ice-covered King Street, they saw four one-legged men on crutches swinging their way toward them—and Amelia knew that she had to *do* something to help, something more than rolling bandages.

"I'd like to stay here and help in the hospitals," she wrote her mother. "I can't bear the thought of going back to school and being so useless."

It meant she couldn't graduate from Ogontz, but she received Mrs. Earhart's permission to drop out.

After taking a crash course in Red Cross First Aid and enlisting in the Voluntary Aid Detachment, she was assigned to the Spadina Military Hospital and became a nurse's aide. Her own account of her duties was modest and understated. "Nurse's aides," she later recalled, "did everything from scrubbing floors to playing tennis with convalescing patients. The patients called us 'sister' and we hotfooted here and there to attend their wants. 'Please rub my back, sister. I'm so tired lying in bed.' Or, 'Won't you bring me ice cream today instead of rice pudding?'

"We were on duty from seven in the morning until seven at night with two hours off in the afternoon. I spent a great deal of time in the diet kitchen and later in the dispensary, because I knew a little chemistry." And she wryly added, "Probably the fact that I could be trusted not to drink up the medical supply of whisky counted more than the chemistry."

Her main effort was devoted to improving the base hospital's cuisine, which, being under the supervision of an English woman, was predictably dreary. Again her reformist tendency cropped up. As tactfully as possible she pleaded the case of the wounded men in the wards for a more varied and imaginative menu with the head dietitian. Her adversary was also a strong-minded female and needed considerable persuasion to add tomatoes to the fare as a change from the invariable parsnips and turnips. "And besides," Amelia would plead, "tomatoes are so much more cheerfuller." There was also a spirited debate over the rice pudding which was always served the men with the evening meal. They groaned at the sight of it. Blancmange with a little cherry or strawberry flavoring was Amelia's prescription. She stayed up all one night to make a batch out of milk and cornstarch and persuaded other nurse's aides to contribute fancy molds, candied cherries and oranges—a triumph which was greeted by cheers in the wards.

Saturday afternoons she and Muriel went riding on horses rented from a stable near the fairgrounds. Often they rode with Canadian Army and Flying Corps officers, who were stationed nearby at Armour Heights.

It was during that winter of 1917-18 that her interest in aviation was awakened.

One of her riding companions was a Captain Spaulding of the Royal Flying Corps, who admired Amelia's Western style of horsemanship and the way she managed a half-broken horse which had once belonged to a cavalry colonel. "Watching the way you ride that horse reminds me of the way I have to fly my plane," Captain Spaulding told her. "Sometimes she goes along smooth as silk and then she gets contrary and bucks a bit just to show off."

He then invited the girls to come out to the airfield and watch him fly. They eagerly accepted but were disappointed when Spaulding cited regulations that forbade him to take them up for a ride. Soon Amelia was spending most of her off-duty hours at the airdrome watching the training maneuvers.

"I remember the sting of the snow on my face," she later wrote, "as it was blown back from the propellers when the training planes took off on skis."

The planes were mostly Curtiss Jennies, Canadian RFC trainers, but when they were piloted skillfully, the grace and speed of their flight held Amelia enthralled. Flying had captured her imagination long before she went up for her first flight. There was a poetry about those tiny sputtering machines, struggling into the air against the harsh northerly winds, that utterly fascinated her.

They made almost as great an impression on her as the suffering she witnessed in the wards of the base hospital. That imprint of endless agony, of wasted and shattered youth, would never leave her mind.

In later years, during the fashionable pacifism of the thirties, she would be stanchly antiwar, not only as a matter of intellectual conviction but because she could not forget the suffering she had seen at Spadina hospital.

"There is no doubt whatever," says her sister Muriel, "that what she saw at Spadina later made her a dedicated pacifist."

She stayed on for almost a year as a nurse's aide, until after the Armistice, November 11, 1918. One matter of pride to her later was the fact that when the great flu epidemic broke out, taking hundreds of thousands of lives in Europe and America, she was still on her feet and was "one of the few volunteers permitted to be on night duty." She was stationed in the pneumonia ward during those grueling weeks and "helped to ladle out medicine from buckets" in the overcrowded hospital.

Working almost around the clock, with only a few hours' sleep snatched at odd intervals, finally caught up with her. She came down with a serious attack of pneumonia. When she had recovered sufficiently to travel, she joined Muriel in Northampton, Massachusetts, where her sister was attending Smith College. Amelia was too restless to dedicate herself wholeheartedly to convalescence and relieved the boredom by taking a course in automobile engine repair, not then regarded as a feminine pursuit. It did not appeal to her as a career, but she felt it might come in handy, somehow.

Her current ambition was to take up a medical career, an interest awakened by her year as a nurse's aide. After a summer spent resting on the shores of Lake George with her sister and mother, the latter planning on joining their father in Los Angeles, where he believed the legal prospects were brighter, she entered Columbia University in New York as a premedical student. Characteristically, she overloaded herself with work. In addition to a full schedule of laboratory and lecture courses at Columbia and its sister school, Barnard, she enrolled as an auditor in other classes. She took on what she called a "luxury course" in French and became fascinated by French poetry.

Her interests were so Protean, so expressive of the intense, driving curiosity which had marked her since childhood, that it was apparent to her friends at Columbia that Amelia would never be able to narrow the range and concentrate on becoming a doctor.

"During the Columbia winter," Marian Stabler, a friend and fellow student, would remember, "she was letting the bacteriology professor inoculate her with experimental serums—a sort of willing guinea pig. She had that nasty abscess under the cheekbone [an infection of the antrum contracted during her Toronto hospital work] which wasn't located for years, but was infecting her system and running her down frightfully. Nobody seemed to be able to figure out what caused the infection, but the professor thought he might be able to help her, so she took millions of bugs in the arm, on the principle that it couldn't make her any worse, and he might learn something scientifically useful."

She and Louise de Schweintz, a Smith graduate whom she had met while convalescing with her sister in Northampton, were protégées of Professor James MacGregor, a biologist, who often invited them to have tea after they helped him clean up the laboratory late in the afternoon. MacGregor said of Amelia, "She grasped the significance of an experiment, mentally assayed the results, and drew conclusions while I was still lecturing about setting up the experiment. She was a most stimulating student. . . . I feel that had Amelia not become caught up in the adventure of flying, she would have found equally challenging frontiers to conquer in the laboratory."

She was too restless and venturesome for anything so confining. Her interests ranged from French poetry to hiking on the Palisades across the Hudson to frequent concert going. "Students in New York," she later reflected, "can get so much with so little if they really wish. The steps in the gallery of Carnegie Hall are really not uncomfortable and I enjoyed many a concert from that locality—after I got used to the smell of garlic." And she explored the Columbia campus with the same curiosity that she investigated the caves in the Missouri bluffs during her girlhood on Quality Hill. "I was familiar with all the forbidden underground passageways which connected the different buildings of the University. I think I explored every nook and cranny possible. I have sat in the lap of the gilded statue which decorates the library steps, and I was probably the most frequent visitor on the top of the library dome. I mean the top."

She also subjected herself to a rigorous self-examination during that year at Columbia and came up with the conclusion that she really wasn't cut out to be a doctor. "It took me only a few months to discover that I probably should not make the ideal physician. Though I liked learning all about medicine, particularly the experimental side, visions of its practical application floored me. For instance, I thought among other possibilities of sitting at the bedside of a hypochondriac and handing out innocuous sugar pellets to a patient with an imaginary illness. 'If you'll take these pills,' I heard myself saying in a professional tone, 'the pain in your knee will be much less, if not entirely eliminated.' This picture made me feel inadequate and insecure. . . ."

At Ogontz she had prepared for college, and at Columbia she had prepared for a career in medicine, but she was still taking compass bearings on what she really wanted to do with her life.

She also withdrew from Columbia because domestic storm signals were flying from the Los Angeles home of her parents. They wrote rather urgently asking her to continue her education in California. Obviously what they wanted was a buffer. Amelia did not much care for the role but told Muriel that she would go home and see if she could keep their parents together. After that, she told Muriel, "I'm going to come back here and live my life."

4
Fledgling

AMELIA went out to California in the summer of 1920 to try the role of peacemaker between her parents. A divorce was in the offing, but possibly her efforts contributed to keeping them together awhile longer. At least her father had finally been cured of his drinking problem. Where the indignation of his late in-laws, the suffering of his wife and children, the disapproval of his various employers had failed, Christian Science had succeeded. Edwin Earhart was now a permanent passenger on the water wagon.

A Christian Scientist whose office was located near Earhart's had converted him, took him to Wednesday night meetings, and by applied Christian Science got his mind off alcohol and onto the teachings of Mary Baker Eddy. Furthermore, he was introduced to a wide circle of fellow worshipers, some of whom brought their legal business to him. This time a modest measure of prosperity did not throw him off balance.

The Earharts were living in a large house on Fourth Street near downtown Los Angeles and rounded out their income by taking in boarders. One of the three young men staying with them was Sam Chapman, a chemical engineer, who was immediately attracted to Amelia. She made it clear enough in letters to her sister that she enjoyed Chapman's company. Both were serious-minded, and it was hardly the typical romance—complete with fast roadsters and hip flasks—of the twenties. Instead of roadhouses or speakeasies, they frequented political meetings. Amelia was strongly liberal-humanitarian in her social and political outlook, and with Chapman as her escort, both roughly dressed, they attended a meeting of the proscribed IWW (International Workers of the World).

By that time, however, she had acquired an overriding interest in aviation. It had fascinated her ever since she had watched the training activities at the RFC field outside Toronto. It became almost an obsession after her father took her to an air show at Long Beach, when she sought information on how much it cost to learn to fly: one thousand dollars. A short time later she went up for the first time from a suburban airfield out on Wilshire Boulevard hemmed in by oil derricks. The pilot was Frank Hawks, who was to hold many speed records.

Amelia immediately signed up for flying lessons. The family budget could not afford that expense, so she took a job at the Los Angeles telephone company. Her instructor was Neta Snook, the first woman to graduate from the Curtiss School of Aviation; later she took more advanced lessons from John Montijo, a former Army instructor (the Air Force was then part of the Signal Corps).

For the first time in her life she felt really free, alive, in her proper element. Airborne, even in one of the rickety trainers then in use, most of them Army surplus, she felt entirely secure, the problems of her earthbound life temporarily eliminated. "From then on," she would recall, "the family scarcely saw me for I worked all week and spent what I had of Saturday and Sunday at the airport a few miles from the town. The trip there took more than an hour to the end of the carline, and then a walk of several miles along the dusty highway. In those days it was really necessary for a woman to wear breeks [breeches] and a leather coat. The fields were dusty and the planes hard to climb into. Flyers dressed the part in semi-military outfits and in order to be as inconspicuous as possible, I fell into the same style." She also cropped her hair. Inconspicuous or not, she loved the costume, reveled in the atmosphere of a dusty airfield with its ramshackle hangars and the wind sock which passed for meteorological expertise.

With an instructor in the rear cockpit ready to grab the controls, she practiced the various aerial maneuvers, takeoffs, and landings in a Curtiss Canuck, a descendant of the wartime Jenny trainer. What seemed to be "stunting" to those on the ground actually, as she later explained, was learning how to cope with emergencies that arose in flight. "The fundamental stunts taught to students are slips, stalls and spins. . . . Loops, barrel rolls and variations and combinations of many kinds are included depending on the instruction desired. . . . A knowledge of some stunts is judged necessary to good flying. Unless a pilot has actually recovered from a stall, has actually put his plane into a spin and brought it out, he cannot know accurately what those acts entail. He should be familiar enough with abnormal positions of his craft to recover without having to think how."

The hazards of stunting admittedly were part of the joy of flying to Amelia Earhart. Perhaps this was because of what veteran pilots observed of her from her first fledgling flights: She was a "natural," the aircraft became an extension of herself, she was coolheaded, and she handled a plane with the same sure, steady hands with which she managed an unruly horse.

Stunting was often merely showing off for the groundlings, but she admitted she had fun performing the barrel rolls, sideslips, Immelmann turns, and other aerial acrobatics. "So much so, in fact, I have sometimes thought that transport companies would do well to have a 'recreation plane' for their pilots who don't have any chance to play in the big transports or while on duty. If a little stunt ship were available, the men could go up 5,000 feet and 'turn it inside out' to relieve the monotony of hours of straight flying."

The exhilaration of soaring into the still smog-free skies over

Los Angeles was so great that Amelia could hardly bear coming back to earth. Once she jumped out of her training plane and exclaimed to her sister Muriel, "It's so breathtakingly beautiful up there I want to fly whenever I can."

Muriel was more earthbound and was not tempted to join in the sport but often went out to the field on Wilshire Boulevard, where the adobe dust rose in clouds whenever there was a takeoff, with a picnic basket for Amelia and her friends. The pilots and mechanics, many of them veterans of the AEF or other World War I air forces, were a rough and ready group, profane and hardbitten, but it was observed that they moderated their language and conduct when the Earhart girls were around.

The only irksome thing was that it took Amelia so many months to earn enough money at the telephone company to pay for enough lessons before she was ready to solo.

When the big day arrived, she was cool and self-confident. Clad in breeches, boots, and a long leather jacket, with the traditional scarf around her neck, she vaulted into the cockpit of a Kinner biplane; a mechanic spun the prop, and she zoomed down the runway with the nonchalance of a veteran. She was on her own now; there was no one to seize the controls if anything went wrong. Such possibilities did not concern her, except as a challenge to be joyfully met. Early in her training, when Neta Snook was her instructor, their Canuck had suffered an engine failure shortly after takeoff. Miss Snook made an emergency landing in a nearby cabbage field. Amelia was so self-possessed that she reached over and cut the switch before the plane touched down.

On her solo flight Amelia took the biplane up to 5,000 feet, maneuvered it expertly for a while, and then came down to make what she later admitted as "an exceptionally poor landing." Most tyros stayed up until their gasoline supply was almost exhausted out of fear of making their first solo landing.

When she jumped out of the plane, a pilot who had been watching told her, "You didn't do anything right but land rottenly." For a student pilot, he meant. "Don't you know you're supposed to be so ground-shy you stay up until the gas tank runs dry?"

Possibly her obsession with flying was partly traceable to the problems always waiting for her when she returned to earth. The family troubles, which made her shy from marrying until much later than most women, were not abated by her presence. They were only increased by financial pressures on her parents. Mrs. Earhart's legacy had dwindled from $45,000 to $20,000 in the past four years.

The Earharts saw an opportunity to rebuild that inheritance when their boarder and Amelia's suitor, Sam Chapman, introduced them to a fellow engineer named Peter Barnes. It developed that Barnes had just taken an option on a Nevada gypsum mine. He and a partner then bought the mining rights to the gypsum deposits on a mountain near the Moapa Indian reservation, with a railroad siding about six miles away. With all the postwar construction going on, there was a ready market for high-grade gypsum. The trouble was, Barnes didn't have the capital to develop his property, though Ute laborers were available at wages of seventy-five cents a day. He needed trucks to carry the gypsum to the rail spur, pumping machinery to drain the quarry, and other heavy equipment.

Mrs. Earhart, with the concurrence of her husband, who had prudently investigated the mine's potential and the character of Barnes and his partner, decided to invest what was left of her legacy, about $20,000, in the gypsum venture. It was a risk, but they were betting on Barnes' proven skill as an engineer and his determination.

Early in 1922 Edwin Earhart and Amelia took a train to Las Vegas to see how Barnes and his Ute laborers were getting along. Barnes met their train in a pickup truck and took them to the quarry, 26 miles up into the mountains. They were amazed at the amount of work he had done; already he was taking gypsum out and trucking it to the railhead.

There was one ominous circumstance: The Ute workers had refused to report that day. There was not a cloud in the sky, but they insisted that the winter rains—with the possibility of flash floods—were coming to the mountains. As always, they were moving to higher ground, knowing how quickly a mountain gully could fill with water and destroy everything in its path.

Barnes refused to accept the native prophecy and insisted the work had to go on. Amelia and her father helped him shovel gypsum into the buckets of the conveyor belt. Later it would be transferred to a truck for the journey down the mountainside.

That afternoon clouds began to appear, then to thicken, and when reports came in that it had begun raining in the higher elevations, Barnes decided they had better evacuate as quickly as possible. Amelia and her father, along with two friends of Barnes who had been helping out, got across the makeshift bridge on the road leading down the mountain just before a fifteen-foot wall of water came roaring down. Barnes was following them with a heavily loaded truck. The torrent tore away the bridge, and Barnes and his truck were swept into the flooded gulch. Later his body was recovered; the next morning the Earharts brought it to Las Vegas in the pickup truck.

The quarry and all its workings were flooded, and there was nothing to be salvaged from the investment. All hopes for the further education of the Earhart daughters were washed away —Muriel's last year at Smith, Amelia's planned continuation of her studies at Columbia.

It was less of a blow to Amelia than to her sister. All that Amelia wanted to do was continue her flying. Both her parents were opposed, but they had brought up their daughters to be independent, and Amelia was a stubborn young woman. How was she to make a career out of flying? Even the most experienced male pilots could barely scratch a living out of stunting before county-fair audiences, racing for slim purses, giving flying lessons, obtaining an occasional contract for flying supplies to a remote mining operation. Practical as she was in most things, Amelia was a wild romantic when it came to airplanes. In any case, as she said later, "I certainly didn't think of my flying [in 1922] as a means to anything but having fun." To pay for that fun, she took up commercial photography after enrolling in a course in that subject at the University of Southern California.

Her parents, though mildly disapproving, were certainly indulgent toward their eldest daughter's obsession with airplanes. They did not flinch too much even after Amelia walked away from two crash landings. Once she had to pancake her plane in a farmer's field during a rainstorm; the plane nosed over on its back, and Amelia hung upside down from her safety belt. Another time she was forced down into a field overgrown with high weeds. Again the plane flipped over, but this time Amelia's safety belt broke, and she was flung out of the cockpit. Neither of the accidents resulted from recklessness or incompetence; they were all part of the hazard of flying in the day of put-put engines not much bigger than a motorcycle's.

At considerable sacrifice, her parents and sister chipped in to buy her a plane on her twenty-fourth birthday, July 24, 1922. It was a Kinner Canary—a small yellow biplane fabricated by William Kinner, a pioneer aircraft designer and a friend of hers at the Wilshire Boulevard airfield. Most of the money for that present came from her mother, out of her share of the proceeds from the recent sale of her parents' house on Quality Hill. Apparently Amelia's close-knit family recognized, or sensed, that flying was going to be more than a hobby with her.

From the few books then available on the subject, from old newspapers and other sources, she began researching the brief but lively history of women in aviation, going back to the lighter-than-air days. Somewhere she acquired a handbill advertising the balloon ascent of Mrs. Graham, "the only female aeronaut," from the Royal Gardens, London, on July 11, 1850. She learned that while the public knew all about the pioneering exploits of the Wright brothers, there was also a Wright sister, Katherine, who turned over her salary as a teacher to her brothers, Orville and Wilbur, to allow them to continue their experiments. "Much of our effort has been inspired by her," one of them said.

So far as Amelia could learn from the records, the first woman to receive a pilot's license was the Baroness de la Roche in 1910 after an adventurous career as an automobile racer. Three years later she was awarded the Coupe Femina for a 160-mile flight that took four hours.

The first American woman to be licensed was a Boston newspaperwoman named Harriet Quimby, in 1911. Louis Blériot had flown across the Channel in 1909, and shortly after qualifying as a pilot, Miss Quimby was determined to be the first woman to make the same flight. A slender, attractive young woman, Miss Quimby made her attempt in a Blériot monoplane. Her costume was gorgeously outlandish, a high-necked blouse and full bloomers fashioned from purple satin, with kid boots laced to her knees. The outfit was topped by goggles, gauntlets, and a long leather coat.

A purple apparition, perhaps, but she managed to fly her monoplane from Deal, England, to Epihen, France. Flying at the 6,000-foot level she ran into heavy clouds and might have strayed off course if she hadn't carried a pocket compass. A few months later, on July 1, 1912, Miss Quimby was killed when her plane crashed during a Boston air show.

The second American woman pilot was Mathilde Moisant, whose brother John operated a flying school on Long Island and managed a troupe of exhibition fliers. After her brother was killed, Mathilde took over the troupe for a brief but exciting aerial career. At an exhibition in Wichita Falls, Texas, she insisted on taking off despite a high wind. The plane crashed on takeoff, but Mathilde was hauled out of the wreckage with singed hair and leggings after the gasoline tank exploded. Her family then insisted that she stop flying and bought her a plantation in Central America as a reward for hanging up her goggles.

Probably the most famous of the prewar female pilots was Ruth Law, who held the third license granted an American woman. More than any other of her sex, until Amelia Earhart's generation came along, she was filled with the competitive spirit. Shortly after Victor Carlstrom attempted a nonstop flight from Chicago to New York, which ended in Erie, Pennsylvania, when a fuel line broke and he was forced down, Ruth Law made a try at the same exploit. In December of 1916 she took off from Grant Park in Chicago, skimming through the Loop at a 200-foot altitude and maneuvering between the taller buildings. Her tank held only 53 gallons, but extra containers filled all the available space in her little Curtiss D.

Navigational aids were at a premium in those days, and the intrepid Miss Law had only a compass and a clock to guide her cross-country. She also carried a barograph which would testify that she had not landed anywhere along the flight.

In an open cockpit, muffled in wool and leather, she stuck it out against the biting winds and the December cold. Five and a half hours later she was forced to land at Hornell, New York— 128 miles farther up the line than Carlstrom—when her gasoline supply was exhausted. She landed in a farmyard, refueled, and doggedly continued the flight to New York City. Her engine began sputtering by the time she reached the Harlem River, and she had to make a dead-stick landing on Governor's Island. Her reception at that military post was an indication of the honors and rewards waiting for the pioneers of aviation. She was greeted by General Leonard Wood and the polar explorers Amundsen and Peary and was given $2,500 and the Aero Club's Medal of Merit as the bands played and the troops paraded.

For several years Miss Law barnstormed the country, but she had retired by the time Amelia was learning to fly.

Another celebrated woman flier of the years preceding World War I was Katherine Stinson, whose brothers were also aviation pioneers and plane builders. She was a tiny girl who weighed about 100 pounds and had to stand up in her cockpit in order to be seen by the airfield crowds when she made one of her record cross-country hops.

Katherine Stinson, as Ruth Law's chief feminine rival, decided she could better Miss Law's distance record. Flying the same route, she also took off from Grant Park in Chicago. She managed to reach Binghamton, New York, and established a new record of 783 miles nonstop, broke her propeller on landing, but carried on to land at a field on Sheepshead Bay. Like other early birds, she used railroad maps to guide her across the country.

Her younger sister, Marjorie, succumbed to the family fascination with airplanes and at the age of eighteen, in 1914, presented herself at the Wright brothers' flying school in Dayton, Ohio. She looked even younger than she was, and the Wrights wouldn't consider accepting her as a student until her parents had telegraphed their consent. Five men were her classmates, and it took six weeks for her to put in enough time behind the dual controls of a training plane to solo.

Marjorie Stinson distinguished herself by acting as an unofficial instructor for the Canadian Royal Flying Corps. She was an accomplished pilot by 1917, when four Canadians sent her a telegram asking if she could teach them to fly well enough to join the air force. She could and did and subsequently trained about fifty others for the same service.

Some very intrepid young women had broken Amelia's path to the American skyways.

One Sunday in October, 1922, Amelia rather mysteriously slipped her sister and father a pair of tickets for an air show to be held at Rogers Field and indicated they might find it interesting.

Temporary bleachers had been set up for the crowd on the field. Shortly after they were seated Muriel and her father heard an announcement on the loudspeaker system: Miss Amelia Earhart was going to try for a new women's altitude record in her Kinner Canary under the auspices of the California Aero Club. A sealed barograph for measuring altitude had been placed in her plane.

She soared to 14,000 feet, a new women's record, before her engine conked out. It was a risky business, venturing almost three miles above the earth in a plane powered by a three-cylinder, sixty-horsepower engine, but she landed safely. She ignored the cheers when she landed and immediately conferred with the mechanics on the field to learn why the engine had quit on her. The spark control lever, they said, had become disconnected during a test run. To her father and sister she explained that she didn't care much about setting new records "except that it will help Bill Kinner sell his planes."

The record, in fact, stood only a few weeks before another woman pilot, Ruth Nichols, later a close friend, climbed to a still higher altitude.

Amelia's competitive sense was well developed by then. Her determination to recapture the women's altitude championship betrayed her into pushing herself and her plane so relentlessly it almost cost her life.

She took the Kinner Canary up into a high battlement of clouds and began flying blind. A dangerous euphoria, something like that which grips deep-sea divers, seized her and kept her pulling back on the stick. As she related, "From the sight of cities and the glistening sea two miles below, I plunged into a rolling bank of clouds. There was snow inside. It stung my face and plastered my goggles." At that point a sensible veteran pilot—if any existed in those days—would have nosed down and abandoned the attempt to set a new record. She climbed to 11,000 feet, at which level the snow turned to sleet, then into dense fog at 12,000 feet.

There were no instruments to guide her, and she had entered a sort of limbo. Later she noted that "human sensations fail when one is thus 'blind.' Deprived of a horizon, a flier may lose the feel of his position in space. Was I flying one wing high? Was I turning? I couldn't be sure. I tried to keep the plane in flying trim, with one wish growing stronger every moment—to see the friendly earth again."

Unwisely, she took a chance, pulled the stick back, and kicked the rudder to send the plane into a spin. Down, down she spiraled through the heavy overcast, letting gravity, a dangerous copilot, take over the controls.

Fortunately she managed to zoom out of the spin at 3,000 feet after the earth became visible again.

Jauntily, but shaking inside, knowing that she would have crashed if her tiny engine had failed to start and pull her out of the spin, she vaulted out of the plane. She took off her helmet and combed her short curly hair with her fingers.

"What the hell were you trying to do?" shouted another pilot, running over to her across the adobe. "You came down like a bullet. Suppose the overcast had closed in completely? You'd have come all the way down, and we'd've had to dig you out in pieces."

"Yes," Amelia replied coolly, "I suppose you would."

5
Doing Good in Boston

*L*ONG in the making, never close to healing despite the best annealing efforts by their daughters, the breach between Amy and Edwin Earhart was deemed irreparable, unbearable, by the summer of 1924. They decided to recognize the hopelessness of staying together and agreed that Edwin should obtain an uncontested divorce while Amy went East with their daughters.

Amelia was persuaded to give up flying, for the time being at least, and accompany her mother and sister to Boston. Muriel and Amelia would complete their education and get teaching jobs. The arrangement also pleased Sam Chapman, who apparently believed that Amelia at last was coming down to earth and was ready for marriage. She sold her much-prized Kinner Canary and bought a Kissel touring car to drive her mother and sister across the country.

Actually, Amelia was biding her time, doing her filial duty, willing to wear skirts and study or teach to please her mother, but with her heart still in the skies, her real ambition aloft in a cockpit. The way she drifted from school to job, back and forth, during the next several years indicated that there was no deep satisfaction in a humdrum existence of educating or being educated. She dropped in at Columbia for a semester, then dropped out again. She taught English to the foreign-born under the University of Massachusetts extension program for helping them to gain U.S. citizenship. She spent the summer of 1925 as a student at the Harvard summer school. Muriel was teaching English in a junior high school and urged her to try the pleasures of instructing the young, but Amelia was too restless—perhaps cognizant that she could never be happy with her feet on the ground—for a teaching career.

A half-dozen years later she would boast that she had held twenty-eight different jobs in her short life and hoped to have two hundred twenty-eight more. "Experiment! Meet new people. That's better than a college education," she declared in 1932. "You will find the unexpected everywhere as you go through life. By adventuring about, you become accustomed to the unexpected. The unexpected then becomes what it really is —the inevitable."

She had to find something more exciting than teaching middle-class children in a middle-class suburb, something that would stretch her capabilities in a new direction.

Early in the autumn of 1926 she decided that settlement-house work might provide the challenge she was looking for. She presented herself at Denison House in Tyler Street, a formerly elegant neighborhood now populated mostly by Italian, Syrian, and Chinese immigrants, with a sprinkling of Irish; it was the second oldest settlement house in Boston. There was a position open for an apprentice social worker which paid $60 a month.

The head of the center was Marion Perkins, who was immediately taken with the applicant. As Miss Perkins later described her, Amelia was "tall, slender, boyish-looking. . . . She had poise and charm . . . before I knew it I had engaged her for halftime work. . . . I liked her quiet sense of humor, the frank direct look in her grey eyes."

Amelia already had her own convictions about the role of a

social worker, though she had never studied sociology in college. "Social work does not begin and end with philanthropy,"
she felt. "Social work to me is essentially education, for it is syn-
onymous with the ability to make adjustments to poverty, illness, illiteracy or any other morbid condition; and in order to
make such an adjustment competently, the first requisite is a
sound education. Social service should be preventative rather
than curative."

The work and the neighborhood were fascinating to her,
especially since most of her experience of American life had
been in the Middle Western middle class (and that went for
Southern California, too, with its strong flavor of the corn
belt). Tyler and the surrounding streets were exotic by comparison, scented by autumn leaves and Oriental spices. "I had
never been privileged to know much about how people other
than Americans lived," she remarked in *The Fun of It*. "Now I
discovered manner and modes very different from those with
which I was familiar. Under my very nose Oriental ideas and
the home-grown variety were trying to get along together. The
first time I saw, sitting on a modern gas stove, one of the native
clay cooking dishes used for centuries by the Syrians, I felt I
was seeing tangible evidence of the blending process." She had
to adjust herself to the Syrian or Chinese adaptation of English.
"The word 'fresh' covered all degrees of misconduct and could
be a slight rebuke or an insult. It was funny to hear of a 'fresh'
baby instead of a naughty one. The Chinese called it 'flesh' but
kept the same meaning."

Among her duties at the settlement house were teaching
classes in English for the foreign-born, both children in the day-
time and adults at night. Her superior, Miss Perkins, recorded
that Amelia was particularly capable in directing prekindergar-
ten classes and both study and games for girls five to fourteen
years old. "She herself made studies of children that show her
keen insight into child life. Here are sentences taken from her
record of a seven-year-old boy. 'Ferris is fond of making experiments of various kinds. How far can a pencil be moved before

it falls? How high can the chairs be piled before spilling? He conceived the idea on a cold day of "warming" his little sister's beads on his father's stove. That the beads were hot enough to burn the child when she put them on was not part of the experiment.' "

Once, rather shyly, she showed Miss Perkins a poem she had written. The first stanza read:

"Courage is the price that Life exacts for granting peace.
The soul that knows it not, knows no release
From little things;
Knows not the livid loneliness of fear,
Nor mountain heights where bitter joy can hear
The sound of wings."

Certainly it was a fair summation of her own philosophy. The "sound of wings"—those of a man-made bird—was still audible in the background of her conscious mind. For the moment, however, the work at Denison House absorbed her time and energies; there was never enough money for the projects planned, and much of the work was carried on by volunteers from the schools and colleges around Boston. "There were sick children who had to be taken to the hospitals and poor mothers who had to have explained to them that hospitals were not dreadful places where their children were imprisoned and tortured by cruel doctors. It is not easy to understand the ways of a new country when one knows nothing of the laws or customs. Half the trouble caused by the so-called 'furiners' is only because no one has taken the trouble to interpret to them the best these United States stand for. . . ."

In less than a year Amelia had shown herself so adept at the work of Denison House that she was promoted to full-time resident worker.

Meanwhile, Sam Chapman had come out from Los Angeles, more hopeful than ever that he could persuade Amelia to marry him. Her sister was certain that she really loved Chapman; they had many interests in common and had known each other for seven or eight years. Chapman got a job as engineer with the Boston Edison Company and was confident that he would be able to argue Amelia into chucking her career. He and Amelia, Muriel, and a young man named Albert Morrissey whom Muriel later married, often drove down to Marblehead to swim, dig clams, and picnic around a driftwood fire on Marblehead Neck.

Chapman was delighted that she had apparently given up flying but was distressed at her decision, when she was appointed resident worker, to move into an apartment on the top floor of Denison House. That would leave little time for him and would all but preclude marriage. He offered to find another job with more regular hours if she would give up social work and pleaded with her to marry him and settle down. They would move into the beautiful old house at Marblehead which he had inherited.

But Amelia wasn't ready to be tied down, couldn't stand the thought of losing her independence. Chapman's offer to find another job only annoyed her. Muriel quoted her as saying, "I don't want to tell Sam what he should do. He ought to know what makes him happiest and then do it, no matter what other people say."

Their semiofficial engagement was soon broken.

Whatever pain that broken romance caused her was deadened by her total dedication to the people of the Tyler Street neighborhood. Their struggles to make their way in a strange and terrifying world seemed much more important than any of her personal problems. One thing that especially concerned her was the fact that many of the children of those hard-pressed families never knew the carefree joys of childhood. Often she loaded a dozen children into her low-slung Kissel, which she called the "yellow peril," and drove them into the country for outings and picnics.

A Syrian boy who attended classes at Denison House was blinded when a kerosene heater exploded in his tenement home. When he was able to leave the hospital, Amelia drove him to the celebrated Perkins Institute on the outskirts of the city three times a week so he could learn to read Braille. Many of the instructors at Perkins were blind themselves, and Amelia was so impressed by the worth of their work that she spent several hours a week as a reader at the institute.

But she still heard the "sound of wings" she had alluded to in her poem. She could never quite forget the exhilaration, the freedom and exalted loneliness of her flights over Los Angeles. She could never feel so vibrantly alive as when she entrusted her life to a wood and canvas contraption and its tiny temperamental engine. Nor was that piercing nostalgia lessened when she learned that the man who bought her Kinner Canary—her "little sandpiper," as she sentimentally called it—had crashed while stunting and lost his life. No doubt that interest was heightened in 1927 when young Charles A. Lindbergh made his solo flight across the Atlantic and became the most admired person in the world; perhaps even then she was wondering why there shouldn't be a female counterpart of Lindbergh.

William Kinner, from whom she had bought her first plane, wrote from Los Angeles asking her to help find someone who could establish a sales agency for his product. One of the people she met while scouting around for an agent was Harold T. Dennison, an architect with a side interest in aviation. Dennison owned a large plot of marshland out near what is now Squantum Naval Air Station and had turned it into a landing field of sorts. He also proposed to form a corporation which would build a commercial airport and persuaded Amelia to join his board of directors.

She began flying again on weekends, mainly to demonstrate the Kinner Canary for prospective buyers.

Having joined the local chapter of the National Aeronautic Association, she decided to attempt to organize a women flyers' association. That effort led to her long and firm friendship with Ruth Nichols, her leading rival, who later noted that her career and Amelia's ran on parallel tracks. "Again and again, Amelia and I planned the same flights at the same time, each without knowledge of the other's intentions. And, an even stranger co-incidence, we had both been interested originally in medical and social service careers." Another curious circumstance was that Amelia Earhart, Ruth Nichols, Jacqueline Cochran, Louise Thaden, and other pioneer birdwomen were all invincibly ladylike, well bred, and well spoken, almost as though they had been carved out by the same cookie cutter, in striking contrast to their male counterparts—with the freakish exception of Lindbergh—who were tough, profane, hard-living types for the most part, the veterans of various wars, gun-smuggling, barnstorming, and similar scuffling.

Miss Nichols, who lived in Rye, New York (where Amelia later settled, another coincidence), received a letter from Amelia on September 15, 1927, inquiring, "What do you think of the advisability of forming an organization composed of women who fly? I wrote to the N.A.A. for a list of F.A.I. [Fédé-ration Aeronautique Internationale] women and find there have been issued twenty-one licenses. Many of these pilots are not active at the present time, some no longer live." She wanted to know whether Miss Nichols thought an organization of FAI licensees could be formed. "Personally," she added, "I am a so-cial worker who flies for sport, and am on the board of directors of an aeronautical concern. I can not claim to be a feminist but do rather enjoy seeing women tackling all kinds of new prob-lems—new for them, that is."

Some months later, Miss Nichols having expressed keen in-terest in the idea, Amelia wrote again suggesting that both ac-tive and inactive (honorary) women flyers be enrolled in the proposed association. "To have a purpose is sometimes a dead-ening thing, but I think, to boost aviation is behind all thought of mine and probably of yours. . . . As to organization, let us have a governing committee of three, you and I and one of the Honoraries. I think we have to be autocratic about officers, at first, in order to start something. One of us should be chairman, and a secretary and treasurer may be elected later. I am writing these details in order that you may have something to criticize, not as rules to be followed as put down. Won't you write me your idea of a letter to be sent, if you approve of the plan? When an idea strikes me, I have very little control, and I fear you will suffer from another broadside like this, if you don't answer soon. Is this full warning?"

Organizational plans, as it turned out, had to wait upon a much more striking event in Amelia Earhart's life. One afternoon in April, 1928, Amelia was rehearsing a group of children for a settlement house play. One of the other Denison House workers interrupted the rehearsal to tell her that there was a telephone call. Amelia replied that she was busy and suggested that the caller be told to try again later. She wondered whether it was another bootlegger offering large sums to fly liquor in from Canada—an offer that had been made several times before.

She tore herself away from the rehearsal only after the caller insisted it was important that he talk to Amelia immediately.

"My name is Railey," the caller informed her. "Captain Hilton Railey."

"Yes?"

"You're interested in flying, I understand," Captain Railey said.

"I certainly am," Amelia briskly retorted.

"Miss Earhart, would you be willing to do something important for the cause of aviation?"

"Such as what?"

"Flying a plane across the Atlantic."

She paused for only a moment. "Yes," she answered. "Who could refuse a chance like that?"

In those few seconds she made herself a candidate for legendary fame.

6
Prospects of Glory

*A*MELIA suspected at first that the call from Captain Railey might be a hoax or practical joke until she checked and found out that he was a respectable Southern gentleman who now headed a public relations firm with offices in New York, Philadelphia, and Boston, with such aerial notables as Sir Hubert Wilkins, Commander Richard E. Byrd, Lincoln Ellsworth, Clarence Chamberlain, and Ruth Nichols among his clients. The pioneers of aviation, always needing to raise funds for their ventures, did not balk at the uses of publicity.

Railey was a man in his early thirties with an adventurous background. The grandnephew of Mrs. Jefferson Davis and an offshoot of the plantation aristocracy, he was born in New Orleans and became a newspaperman in his native city, Philadelphia, and New York. He served in the Army as a captain in the World War. In 1920 he was sent to newly independent Poland in the dual role of correspondent for the New York *Evening Mail* and emissary of Prince Lubomirski, the Polish minister to the United States, to observe the victory of the Polish Army against invading forces from Soviet Russia. That assignment had been arranged by George Palmer Putnam, whom he had met and become friendly with during his military service. The ultimate object was to be a book about modern Poland, which Putnam would publish.

On a business trip to New York late in April, 1928, Railey dropped in at Putnam's office. The latter suggested that Railey investigate a report Putnam had heard that a wealthy woman had bought Byrd's tri-motored Fokker and planned to fly the Atlantic.

What was Putnam's interest in the matter, Railey had inquired.

"Hell," Putnam replied, "if it's true we'll crash the gate. It'd be amusing to manage a stunt like that, wouldn't it? Find out all you can. Locate the ship. Pump the pilots. Chances are they know all about it. Maybe there's nothing to it. I don't give a God damn one way or the other. Suit yourself. But let me know what you pick up. Telephone me if it's hot." *

The "gate-crashing" suggested by Putnam was soon accomplished. Captain Railey hurried back to Boston and before midnight had tracked down the information that Byrd's Fokker was being refitted with floats at the East Boston airport. He scouted around town until he found a couple of out-of-town fliers, Wilmer Stultz and Lou Gordon, at the Copley Plaza.

Stultz was "tight and talkative," as Railey later recalled, and admitted that he was preparing for a transatlantic flight under hush-hush conditions. In an unguarded moment, however, Stultz let it slip that a man named David T. Layman was his contact with the group sponsoring the flight. With that name, Putnam and Railey were enabled to solve the mystery and penetrate the secrecy surrounding the projected flight. They also managed to persuade the sponsors to allow them to take over the arrangements.

Of all that backstage maneuvering, Amelia knew nothing the afternoon she went over to interview Railey with Marion Per-

---

* Recounted by Railey in his memoir, *Touch'd with Madness,* New York, 1938.

kins at her side. She did learn that she was being seriously considered for a well-financed venture to fly the Atlantic. An essential ingredient of the plan was that a woman, preferably a flier herself, accompany the flight, though a male pilot would be at the controls.

Ocean-hopping had fevered the public imagination for the past decade. Aviation enthusiasts regarded such flights as advancing the air age, aside from their adventurous aspects. The tallest headlines of the twenties were reserved for the transocean fliers, beginning in 1919 when Lieutenant Commander Cummings Read and a five-man crew flew a U.S. Navy amphibian to the Azores and Portugal. The transpacific flight of the *Southern Cross,* a big flying boat, was another stirring achievement. The most exciting event of that decade of many first-time achievements in long-range aviation was Lindbergh's solo flight to Paris in May of 1927.

Just after the Lindbergh flight, Mrs. Frederick Guest of London, whose husband had served in the wartime Air Ministry under Lloyd George, decided that it was time a woman flew the Atlantic. She bought the tri-motored Fokker *Friendship* from Commander Byrd for that purpose. Mrs. Guest was American-born, Amy Phipps of Pittsburgh before her marriage into the British establishment. She was also an heiress. Though a trifle dumpy, middle-aged, and looking more like a dowager-presumptive than an adventuress, she had cast herself in the role of a "Lady Lindy," whose flight from the United States to England would foster goodwill between the countries of her birth and her adoption.

Her grown children talked Mrs. Guest out of risking her own neck on such a chancy proceeding, but she insisted the flight must be made. She would finance it, and "an American girl of the right image" would take her place aboard the *Friendship.* The public relations aspect of the flight was emphasized throughout; hullabaloo was more important than any scientific advances; it was Mrs. Guest's money, and her purpose, Anglo-American solidarity, had to be served.

For that reason her representatives in America had to be very careful to choose a young woman, a "Lady Lindy," whose appearance and personality would please the somewhat imperious backer in London. Something like a movie talent-scouting hunt ensued. Railey was chief scout. Whatever candidates he raked up would be interviewed by an all-male panel consisting of George Palmer Putnam, David T. Layman, and John S. Phipps. Putnam was the head of the long-established book-publishing firm of G. P. Putnam's Sons in New York. Layman was Mrs. Guest's attorney, and the third member of the jury was her brother. They would have to approve of the successful candidate.

In Boston Railey sought advice from retired Rear Admiral Reginald K. Belknap, who told him, "I know a young social worker who flies. I'm not sure how many hours she's had, but I do know she's deeply interested in aviation and a thoroughly fine person. Call Denison House and ask for Amelia Earhart."

From his first glimpse of Miss Earhart, Railey was certain he'd found the right girl; she was young (twenty-nine), competent-looking, coolheaded enough to ask for his "personal references" before he could ask for hers. Best of all, she looked enough like Charles Lindbergh to be his sister, with the same tousled blond hair, shyness, modesty, and all-American grin, and underlying them the same hard-rock sense of purpose. At first sight Railey was convinced that she was "qualified as a person, if not as a pilot."

Railey was also impressed by her poker face when he suddenly asked, "How would you like to be the first woman to fly the Atlantic?"

As he recalled, "Only a flicker in her cool eyes betrayed the excitement this question must have aroused; calmly she asked for details—whatever I was at liberty to tell her. While I was certain in my own mind that she'd prove acceptable to Mrs. Guest, whose name I withheld, I was compelled to add that of course I could advance no such guarantee. It developed that

Miss Earhart had owned several planes and had flown more than five hundred hours. . . . At the time, however, she was unable to fly with the aid of instruments alone, and her experience with tri-motored ships had been inconsequential. With intense interest I observed and appraised her as she talked. Her resemblance to Colonel Lindbergh was so extraordinary that I couldn't resist the impulse to ask her to remove her hat. She complied, brushing back her naturally tousled, wind-swept hair, and her laugh was infectious. . . . Most of all I was impressed by the poise of the boyish figure at my desk. There was warmth and dignity in her manner, her speech." Amelia Earhart, he felt, was not merely the "norm" of American women but their "sublimation."

It was only later that Captain Railey reflected, in a newspaper article, on the consequences of his choice, which transformed her "from an obscure social worker, absorbed in the lives of polyglot gamins at a Boston settlement house, to a world figure in aviation and the honored guest of kings and queens."

He wondered why she had allowed herself to be recruited when "even to her it must have seemed a stunt without constructive benefit to the aeronautical industry" and why afterward she went on risking her life for records and newspaper headlines. His answer was that she was driven on by internal and external pressures. "She was caught up in the hero racket that compelled her to strive for increasingly dramatic records, bigger and braver feats that automatically insured the publicity necessary to the maintenance of her position as the foremost woman pilot in the world. She was a victim of an era of 'hot' aeronautics that began with Lindbergh and Byrd and that shot 'scientific' expeditions across continents, oceans, and polar regions by dint of individual exhibition." But all those facets of the "hero racket" were invisible the day of that first interview. He shot a series of practical questions at her, rapid fire, as she recalled in *The Fun of It*:

Was I willing to fly the Atlantic?

In the event of disaster would I release those in charge from all responsibility?

What was my education—if any?

How strong was I?

How willing?

How much flying experience?

What would I do after the flight?

Railey apparently was satisfied with her answers. She told him she had five hundred hours in the air, and though there would be a male pilot and a mechanic, she hoped to take a turn at the controls. She also admitted that she had not learned to fly by instruments and that she had never handled a plane with more than one engine.

The feminist in her must have flinched slightly when Railey informed her that the pilot would be paid ($20,000) and also the mechanic ($5,000), but her only recompense would be the privilege of making the flight. Even the fees from any newspaper stories she might write about her experience would have to be turned over to the backer.

She was then dispatched to New York for an appearance before the Putnam-Layman-Phipps screening committee. Putnam was the chief inquisitor, his qualifications being the fact that he was the publisher and personal friend of Lindbergh (who authored the best-selling *We*) and others associated with the world of adventure and exploration.

The interview, she reflected later, "found me in a curious situation. If they did not like me at all, or found me wanting in too many respects, I would be deprived of the trip. If they liked me too well, they might be loath to drown me. It was, therefore, necessary for me to maintain an attitude of impenetrable mediocrity. . . ."

Because of Mrs. Guest's insistence on secrecy, Amelia was given few details of the flight plan. She did not know when the *Friendship* would take off, who was financing the venture, who would pilot the plane. So far as the press was concerned, the trimotored Fokker *Friendship* was still owned by Commander Byrd and being prepared for South Pole exploration. On returning to Boston and Denison House, Amelia told Miss Perkins, regarding her meeting with Putnam, Layman, and Phipps, that they had questioned her for about an hour "about my education, and work, and hobbies. I had the feeling they liked me, but, as they did not minimize the hazards of the trip, maybe that isn't good, because they may not want to put me in a situation where I may be dropped in the cold Atlantic's Davy Jones' locker. I realized that they were making me talk to see whether I dropped my 'g's' or used 'ain't,' which I'm sure would have disqualified me as effectively as failing to produce a pilot's license."

Two days later Amelia got a letter from Layman saying she had been selected for the flight and enclosing a contract embodying the terms Hilton Railey had outlined. Fame, if any, would be her only recompense. Commander Richard Byrd would be technical consultant for the flight and pick the pilot and mechanic. Technically, Amelia would be in command and make the decisions once the *Friendship* was on its way across the Atlantic.

With the flight scheduled for mid-June, Amelia wrote Hilton Railey a rather touching letter on May 2: "It is very kind of you to keep me informed, as far as you are able, concerning developments of the contemplated flight. As you may imagine, my suspense is great indeed.

"Please do not think, however, that I hold you responsible in any way for my own uncertainty. I realize that you are now, and have been from the first, only the medium of communication between me and the person or persons who are financing the enterprise. For your own satisfaction may I add here that you have done nothing more than present the facts of the case to me. I appreciate your forbearance in not trying to 'sell' the idea and should like you to know that I assume all responsibility for any risks involved."

The letter tells us something significant about the young woman who wrote it. She was being exceedingly thoughtful, of course, in whitewashing Railey's conscience beforehand in case the *Friendship*'s flight ended in death and disaster. But it was also an indication of her desperate need for fame and distinction, the same drive that propelled her into taking a three-cylinder-engine plane up 14,000 feet only weeks after she had soloed for the first time. She was still the "girl who walks alone," possessed of intense pride, and deep down perhaps she was trying to prove something to the people who had pitied her, during her most impressionable years, for being the daughter of a drunken failure.

In the next several weeks she learned a bit more about the flight and the reasons for secrecy. "Once the world knew," she later recorded (in *20 Hrs. 40 Min., Our Flight in the Friendship*), "we should be submerged in a deluge of curiosity making it impossible to continue the preparations in orderly fashion. Then, too, it would do no good to aviation to invite discussion of a project some accident might delay. Actually the pontoon equipment on this type of plane was experimental, and no one could tell in advance whether or not it would prove practicable. Another objection was the possibility of instigating a 'race,' which no one wanted. . . . By our example we did not want to risk hurrying ill-prepared aspirants into the field with possibly tragic results."

Finally she was taken out to the hangar in East Boston, near the fog-shrouded waters of the harbor, for her first look at the *Friendship*. The big monoplane, German-built and a descendant of the bombers used by the Luftwaffe in World War I, was jacked up in the shadow of the hangar. "Mechanics and welders worked nearby on the struts for the pontoons that were shortly to replace the wheels. The ship's golden wings, with their spread of seventy-two feet, were strong and exquisitely fashioned. The red orange of the fuselage, though blending with the gold, was chosen not for artistry but for practical use. If we had come down orange could have been seen further than any other color."

The plan called for the *Friendship* to be flown to Trespassey Bay, Newfoundland, from which it would hop off for England. After the pontoons were fitted, it was taken on test hops over Boston Harbor to determine its load capability (it was to be equipped with two extra gas tanks holding 900 gallons) and the precision of its instruments.

Amelia finally met the two men with whom she would share the adventure. The pilot would be Wilmer Stultz, a sawed-off, blond, blue-eyed young man of German-American ancestry like Amelia—and with psychological problems that unpleasantly, anxiously reminded Amelia of her father. Bill Stultz was a highly skilled pilot, navigator, and radio operator, a combination of talents rarely found but absolutely essential on the *Friendship* flight. His addiction to the brandy bottle was well known, but there were few pilots of that day, Lindbergh again the exception, who weren't hard drinkers. Amelia was assured that Stultz was OK once he had his hands on the controls, but even a twenty-seven-year-old can be handicapped by a blinding hangover. He was two years younger than Amelia, had served with the 634th Aero Squadron during the war, then had joined the Navy and flown seaplanes from Pensacola from 1919 to 1922. Since then he had taken forty planes to Brazil for Curtiss and instructed Brazilians in how to fly them, had been a test pilot, and had bounced around as a member of the Gates Flying Circus.

Lou Gordon, the mechanic, was twenty-six years old, a Texan without drinking problems. He was also Army-trained and had been a mechanic on the Handley Page bombers which sank two obsolete battleships off the Virginia capes in 1921 as part of General Billy Mitchell's futile campaign to convince the U.S. General Staff of the lethal worth of airpower. After being discharged from the Army in 1926, Gordon had worked for the Philadelphia Rapid Transit Air Service, serving as mechanic on

Fokker trimotors like the *Friendship* flying passengers between Philadelphia, Washington, and Norfolk.

For more than two weeks Amelia and her colleagues studied the weather reports almost hourly, waiting for a break in the pattern which made it stormy around Boston when it was clear in the mid-Atlantic, and vice versa. The waiting got on everyone's nerves, especially Stultz's. His drinking alarmed everyone, but Lou Gordon, an old friend of Stultz's and well acquainted with his reactions to the tension of waiting, assured them the pilot would be all right once they were on their way. George Putnam and Hilton Railey did their best to distract Amelia by taking her on drives into the country, dining with her nightly, and taking her to see Eva Le Gallienne in *The Good Hope*.

Toward the end of May Amelia learned how tricky flying an amphibian was, how sea and weather conditions had to be just right for a takeoff. Twice in the waning days of the month Amelia, Stultz, and Gordon met at 3:30 A.M. in the lobby of the Copley Plaza, where the two men were staying, and set off for the East Boston airport with packs of sandwiches, Thermos bottles, and other gear for the flight to Newfoundland. Each time a tugboat took them out to *Friendship*. They couldn't take off either time because the fog was too thick and there wasn't enough wind to provide lift for their wings.

In a rather somber mood, Amelia wrote two short letters to her parents which were to be opened in the event that the *Friendship* didn't make it. To her father she wrote, in part, "I have no faith that we'll meet anywhere again, but I wish we might." To her mother: "Our family tends to be too secure. My life has really been very happy and I didn't mind contemplating its end in the midst of it."

On June 3 the weather reports from New York, from Britain, and from ships at sea indicated the following morning would be propitious for the first leg of the flight. Once again the trio took off from T Wharf for the *Friendship*, riding on its pontoons in a gentle swell. The weather was clear, and there was a fairly brisk southeast wind.

In a few minutes, with Stultz and Gordon in the cockpit, Amelia crouched just behind them in the cabin to watch the airspeed indicator, they taxied out into the harbor. Twice Stultz gave the plane the gun and it skimmed across the waters, but the *Friendship* was unwieldy with its extra 900 gallons of gasoline. On the third try, it began to lift off. Amelia watched the airspeed indicator intently, saw the needle climb to thirty miles an hour, then forty, fifty, fifty-five, sixty . . . and they were gaining altitude. The two outboard engines sputtered from the dousing of salt water they had received.

Amelia busied herself keeping the logbook. At 7 A.M. she recorded: "Slim [Gordon] has the controls and Bill [Stultz] is tuning in. He has been getting our position. I squat on the floor next to the motion picture camera with my feet in a dunnage bag. There is one man's shoe in the passageway between the gas tanks. It looks odd, but no one cares about its out-of-placedness."

Just about then, Putnam and Railey were passing on the news to press associations and newspapers that the *Friendship* had taken off on the first leg of a flight to England with the first woman ever to fly the Atlantic. From that moment Amelia was a celebrity and would be surrounded by its pleasures and perils until her death.

At 7:30 A.M. she wrote in the logbook: "Ninety-six miles out (1 hour). 2500 feet. Bill shows me on the map that we are near Cash's Ledge. We cannot see anything (if there is anything to see) as the haze makes the visibility poor. The sun is blinding in the cockpit and will be, for a couple of hours. Bill is crouching by the hatchway, taking sights."

At 8:45 they approached the coast of Nova Scotia, well pleased that they were averaging 114 miles an hour with the help of a tail wind. "What a jagged coast," Amelia noted in the log. "There are few roads. Many little houses nestle in the woods seemingly out of communication with anything for miles. One can see deeply into the water and mark shoals and currents. What an easy way to see what are bugaboos for surface craft. . . . The ship flies smoothly, but I know a smaller one would be tossed about. . . . Our shadow skims over the tree-tops. The people whom I cannot see are probably used to the sight and sound of strange planes. . . . The motors are humming sweetly."

So sweetly that they lulled her to sleep. When she awoke, they were flying into a heavy fogbank off Halifax. "Since I last wrote we have circled the harbor [of] Halifax twice and slipped to a landing. Bill went 30 miles beyond and found fog to the treetops, so came back to the clearing here. The natives are swarming to the shore and several dinghies are coming out. Bill and Slim are going over to the land and get reports with the hope we can go on later. I am to stay aboard now, as we all are, later, if there is a chance of continuing. The mournful sound of the fog horn disturbs my peace and hope. I hardly think we could take off here even without fog, as there is no wind at all. Well, anyway, I'd rather visit Halifax this way than any other I can think of. . . ."

Stultz and Gordon returned to the *Friendship* with the latest weather reports. They indicated the weather was closing in, but Stultz decided to try to make Trespassey Bay that day. Halifax was only halfway on the first leg. But they were delayed while Gordon soldered a broken primer. Stultz, knowing the fog would be even thicker along the Newfoundland coast up ahead, decided they would have to spend the night in or around Halifax. Reporters and photographers swarmed around while they tried to settle in at a hotel in Dartmouth. Next morning, before they took off, Amelia sampled their publicity in the Halifax papers and found the first taste of journalistic fame to be slightly disturbing, the "strange assertions they made about us all" a trifle upsetting. She could not recognize herself or her companions in what the reporters wrote about them.

Her doubting mood stayed with her as Stultz took the *Friendship* aloft for the rest of the flight to Trespassey Bay. Looking out the window, Amelia saw a small steamer off to the starboard. "I wonder," she wrote in the logbook, "if she knows who we are. I wonder if we know."

It was a smooth flight, and "weather conditions were so nearly ideal that had it not been necessary to refuel, we should have passed Newfoundland by entirely and continued on our way eastward." Around noon they lunched off the food which had been prepared two days before by the Copley Plaza in Boston. "The tactical error was putting all the ham sandwiches on the top layer. We never got beyond them. Later, to our chagrin, we discovered that below there were similar layers of delicious chicken and tongue sandwiches, hard boiled eggs and much beside. We never had the courage to determine exactly what else there might have been."

Shortly after she reflected that the "sea looks like the back of an elephant," the coast of Newfoundland came into view. Just after 3 P.M. they glided down onto the waters off Trespassey. Almost immediately, they were surrounded by a flotilla of small boats and an almost hysterical unofficial welcoming committee of Newfoundlanders. It looked like a maritime rodeo, with the boatmen hurling ropes at the *Friendship,* Gordon out on a pontoon trying to ward them off, and Stultz cursing fervently because the ropes might foul his propellers.

They finally managed to get ashore, just before a howling gale swept in from the sea. The next day Gordon busied himself with repairs to the Fokker, and Stultz, who could not abide the tension of waiting, fretted and paced. Amelia explored the little fishing village with its frame houses and whitewashed fences. "I could enjoy myself were it not for the anxiety about a takeoff . . . and the disgusting news of publicity. Every few minutes a telegraph operator patters over and hands me a telegram from some one. Some are lovely, and others disturb me greatly. The latest says Boston papers carry a story I went to recoup fallen fortunes of family." Back in Boston her mother and sister learned the news that Amelia would fly the Atlantic from the newspapers: GIRL PILOT DARES THE ATLANTIC. Before they could get over the shock they were surrounded by reporters and photographers. Mrs. Earhart grimly refused to be interviewed, stating firmly that "in my day nice people had their names in the paper only when they were born, married, and died."

She received a telegram from Amelia in Trespassey: KNOW YOU WILL UNDERSTAND WHY I COULD NOT TELL PLANS OF FLIGHT. DON'T WORRY. NO MATTER WHAT HAPPENS IT WILL HAVE BEEN WORTH THE TRYING. LOVE, AMELIA.

Amelia and her companions stayed with a family in one of the larger houses at Trespassey. They had hoped to be able to take off for England in two or three days, but the weather was against them. "The wind held the key to our problems," as Amelia explained in *20 Hrs. 40 Min.* "For three days it blew briskly from the northwest. This was ideal for the flight itself, but far from ideal locally, as it stirred up such sea it was impossible to load the gasoline with safety. What's more, Bill feared that the heavy weight of the load left on board the *Friendship* might seriously injure it as it was buffeted about in the rough water."

They were stalled, as it turned out, for thirteen nerve-grating days.

Amelia, always strong-nerved, busied herself with walking along the beaches, reading (*The Story of the Titanic,* one of the few books available, the great liner having struck an iceberg and sunk off the Newfoundland coast), and playing cards with Gordon. The tall, handsome Texan was equally calm about the delays. The problem was the high-strung Bill Stultz, who again resorted to the brandy bottle. On June 7 she wrote in her log, "The men are simply great under the strain"—but that was only for the record. Stultz, in fact, was close to cracking up—a possibility the flight's backers had foreseen by keeping a standby pilot, Lou Gower, waiting in Boston to take his place if necessary.

That decision would have to be made by Amelia. "The hole in Bill's armor," wrote George Putnam (in *Soaring Wings*) from later conversations with Amelia, "was his tendency to veer off to alcohol to dull progressively the ennui of inaction. I suppose no more ironic difficulty could have risen up to plague a girl who never drank herself, hence knew little about drinkers and the technique—if any—of handling them."

The real irony, of course, was that Amelia knew all about drinkers from experience with her father. She also knew there was no way to cope with a man determined to drink. Her best hope was that the weather would take a favorable turn and they could take off for England before Stultz was racked up by a combination of nerves and alcohol.

Later she told Putnam that she almost gave up on Stultz. "The time came," Putnam related from conversations with her, "when she was almost resolved to send for help. She considered asking us to replace Stultz. . . . But AE was a scrupulously fair person, and she knew that she could not do that without great damage to Stultz; knew also that any last-minute switch might well bring the whole project tumbling down about her. How could she be sure that we—Layman and I—who knew her only slightly could trust her judgment if she did appeal to us? How could she know that we'd not simply think that here was a girl whose inexperience had caught up with her, or whose courage had failed, looking frantically for a way out?"

Amelia decided to take a big-sisterly tack: She was two years older and stood two or three inches above the runtish Stultz. Several times she persuaded him to go fishing, eeling, or hiking along the rocky coast with her and leave the bottle behind. Each time, Stultz either produced a bottle hidden on his person and had to be led back to Trespassey or would suddenly start walking back to the village.

His alcoholic whims became progressively more dangerous. In one paroxysm he insisted that Gordon row him out to the *Friendship*. Despite Gordon's pleas, he clambered aboard and began taxiing wildly around the harbor, endangering various fishing boats and running so close to the rocks he almost ripped off the pontoons. Finished with that sport he then ordered Gordon to calk the seams of the pontoons despite the fact there was a choppy sea running. When they returned ashore, Gordon was in a raging temper and declared he would catch the next boat back to Boston, but Amelia managed to persuade him not to quit.

A dozen days went by, with the tension becoming almost unbearable, yet in her official account Amelia would tactfully assert that her most outstanding memories of Trespassey were "the lovely hooked rugs and the excellent trout streams of Newfoundland."

On the evening of June 16 Amelia and Lou Gordon were playing rummy in the front parlor of the house where they were staying. Overhead they could hear Stultz staggering around his room and swearing to himself. Would he ever sober up, they wondered, or was it time to telegraph the backers to have Lou Gower sent up to replace him? They agreed that Stultz was the better pilot of the two, and maybe they'd wait another day before deciding what to do.

They were playing a last round when the doorbell jangled. A messenger from the telegraph office was at the door. He brought a message from New York saying the New York weather forecaster, whose reports they had chiefly been relying on, finally announced that he could promise fair weather over the Grand Banks and the North Atlantic for the next forty-eight hours.

"What about Bill?" Amelia asked Gordon.

"He'll come around."

"Will he be able to fly?"

"Once he gets in the cockpit and instinct takes over. . . ."

Amelia slept fitfully that night, was the first up in the morning, and woke up her two companions.

Gordon got Stultz on his feet somehow, applied cold water outside and hot coffee inside. Even so, Amelia and Gordon almost had to carry the little man down the steep rocky path from the house to the waterfront. They stuffed him into the *Friendship*'s cockpit; he stared blearily at the sunlit waters of the harbor, and they could only hope for the best.

Gordon kept reassuring Amelia that Stultz would be all right once they were under way, but Amelia kept thinking of all those hours of flying ahead. And not only the actual flying but doing the navigating and operating the radio. The prospects seemed even dimmer when she searched around the back of the plane and found that Stultz had stashed a brandy bottle, though Gordon claimed that Stultz never took a swig when he was at the controls. Amelia decided not to take a chance and dumped the bottle over the side.

Now the problem was taking off, getting up the necessary speed on pontoons to lift three tons into the air. They had already jettisoned all the excess baggage and reduced the extra gasoline carried in the two tanks behind the cockpit from 900 to 700 gallons, a fuel margin so slender that Stultz thought they might have to come down along the Irish coast. The only food they brought was scrambled-egg sandwiches, coffee, a few oranges, chocolate, and a bottle of malted milk tablets, plus five gallons of water. They had no clothing except that which they wore.

Three times Stultz taxied over the harbor waters at maximum speed, struggling to get the Fokker into the sky; the plane vibrated under the effort until it seemed all the fittings would be shaken loose. On the fourth pass the *Friendship* finally lurched off the choppy surface of Trespassey Bay, the engines sputtered from their intake of salt water but achieved a steady roar at last, and the airspeed dial pointed to 60 mph. They gained altitude, shook themselves free of land and sea, and headed for the horizon.

7
Landfall

THE chances were that by dawn the next day they would be either international heroes or dead. Amelia Earhart may well have been more reconciled to the second possibility than the first; certainly the first intimations of fame had not been very comforting. Undoubtedly she was possessed by a more than normal drive for recognition and achievement, but more than anything else she wanted to participate actively in the exciting progress of aviation. Thus when the *Friendship* finally made it into the skies off Newfoundland, she was already concentrating on the job at hand: the logbook. A man's jottings would have been matter-of-fact, but Amelia saw things with the eye of a thwarted poet.

She noted airspeeds, altitudes, sky and sea conditions, but she also scribbled down what would have seemed to a veteran airman her wayward, feminine impressions. Off Cape Race the view below was fleeced with fog, and she wrote in the log, "I know Dunsany would like to see the world above the earth. Irish fogs have been described in detail, and their bilious effect, and their fairies and their little people. But no one has written of a bird's-eye view of one from an imaginative eye."

They had taken off shortly after 11 A.M. on June 17, and by noon Bill Stultz's eyes had cleared and his hands were steady on the controls. He performed all his three-in-one functions efficiently. It was almost incredible how he pulled himself together once he was free of the earth. Amelia could only congratulate herself (and Gordon) on sticking with him.

Soon they ran into a line storm and bucked strong head winds and pelting rain. Then the horizon cleared, and Amelia was able to confide to the log, "140 m.p.h. now. Wonderful time. Temp. 52. The heater from cockpit warms the cabin too. . . . Bill says radio is cuckoo. He is calling now. . . . I have just uncurled from lying on Major Woolley's suit for half an hour. . . . There is nothing to see but churned mist, very white in the afternoon sun. . . . I have et a orange. . . . "

She crouched at the chart table and spent most of her time staring out the small square window nearby. The role of passenger was discomfiting, and she may already have been thinking of making this flight solo. When she wasn't observing and taking notes, she slipped into the cockpit behind the two men and watched how they coaxed the best possible performance out of the *Friendship*. If Amelia ever flew the Atlantic alone, she would have to acquire the combined skills of Bill Stultz and Lou Gordon, and they were the best in the business.

At 4:15 P.M. they were still riding out the drifts of fog and cloud with the sea barely visible. Stultz began climbing above the 4,000-foot altitude to surmount the overcast. By radio he contacted a British ship below and got their bearings. "I do believe we are getting out of the fog," she observed. "Marvellous shapes in white stand out, some trail shimmering veils. The clouds look like icebergs in the distance. It seemed almost impossible to believe that one couldn't bounce forever on the packed fog we are leaving. The highest peaks of the fog mountains . . . are tinted pink, with the setting sun. The hollows are grey and shadowy. . . . We are 1096 miles out. . . . The view is too vast and lovely for words. I think I am happy—sad admission of scant intellectual equipment. I am getting housemaid's knee kneeling here at the table gulping beauty. . . ."

Soon nightfall blotted out the view, and Amelia dined off a handful of malted-milk tablets. There was little talk among the three; all were intent on their jobs. The only light came from the illuminated radium dials on the instrument panel. The only sound was of the steady drumming of the engines. So far it had been a marvelously smooth flight, with all the equipment functioning perfectly.

". . . A night of stars. North the horizon is clear cut. To the south it is a smudge. The exhausts send out glowing meteors. How marvelous is a machine and the mind that made it. I am thoroughly occidental in this worship.

"Bill sits up alone. Every nerve and muscle alert. Many hours to go. Marvelous also. . . ."

For hours they had been flying by instruments, rising to the 11,000-foot level, with nothing on which they could take a bearing. Unvoiced but nagging, there was the fear that they might be far off course, lost in an endless blur of fog and cloud. It got so cold in the cabin that Amelia gratefully climbed into the fur-lined flying suit lent her by Major Woolley of Boston. They had been in the air for more than sixteen hours and had a fuel supply for only four or five hours left. If Stultz's navigation was on the mark, they should soon be approaching the Irish and English coasts. If not . . . but no one spoke of that.

As dawn flushed the skies ahead of them, they began descending, venturing back into the fog and mist. "Going down fast. It takes a lot to make my ears hurt. 5000 [feet] now. Awfully wet. Water dripping in window. Port motor coughing. Sounds as if all motors were cutting. Bill opens her wide to try to clear her. Sounds rotten on the right. . . . Fog awful. Motors better, but not so good. . . . We are going to go into, under or over a storm. I don't like to, with one motor acting the way it does. . . ."

Finally, with great relief, they rode out the murk and turbulence, and at the 3,000-foot level they caught sight of the sea below. Amelia's jubilation was evident in her jottings: "Himmel! The sea! We are 3000. Patchy clouds. We have been jazzing from 1000 to 5000 where we now are, to get out of the clouds. At present there are sights of blue and sunshine, but everlasting clouds are always in the offing. The radio is dead."

But they still didn't know where they were. Relying on dead reckoning, they decided that they should be catching a glimpse of the Irish coast any minute now, but there was nothing but sea ahead and below. The fuel supply would allow them not much more than an hour in the air. " 'Mess,' " she later wrote, "epitomized the blackness of the moment. Were we beaten? We all favored sticking to the course. We had to. With faith lost in that, it was hopeless to carry on. Besides, when last we checked it, before the radio went dead, the plane had been holding true."

Suddenly they sighted the big luxury liner furrowing the seas below—the *America.* They circled the ship, tried frantically to get the radio operating again so they could receive their exact position.

Finally, in desperation, Amelia wrapped a note around an orange, tied it with silver string, and placed it in a paper bag. An amateur bombardier for the moment, she dropped the message through the hatch, watched it zoom away in the slipstream. There was a hurried conference on the possibility of making a forced landing near the *America,* but Stultz judged the seas were too rough. They circled the ship again and returned to their original course.

Down below, on the bridge of the *America,* Captain Friend and his first officer had watched the approach of the *Friendship* through their binoculars.

"What's that aircraft?" Captain Friend asked. "Why's she flying so low?"

"Looks like a reconnaissance plane," his first officer speculated.

"It can't be one of ours," the captain remarked, "so it must be the Royal Navy's. They're certainly taking a lot of interest in us."

"My God," the first officer exclaimed, pointing to the brown object dropped by the *Friendship* which plummeted into the water of the *America*'s bow, "we're being bombarded!"

Still unaware that they had been buzzed by a plane from the American shore, they watched the *Friendship* continue on its way eastward.

One hour's fuel supply left, Gordon announced after making a check of the gauges. The mechanic, probably trying to reassure Amelia, came back to her post in the cabin and nonchalantly chewed on a sandwich.

Down below they sighted several small fishing boats, which indicated land could not be far away.

They strained their eyes, quartering the misty horizon for a glimpse of the land mass that must be ahead.

The ceiling had lowered to 500 feet, and they were almost skimming the rough seas below.

Suddenly a blue shadow loomed through the mist—land or another cloud bank.

It was Gordon who shouted first: "Land!"

In a moment the coastline assumed definition. They still didn't know whether they were approaching Ireland or England but agreed it looked like what they imagined an English coast would be. None of them, incidentally, had ever been farther east than Boston before.

The *Friendship* skirted the cliffs while its occupants studied the roadways, pastures, and hedgerows below. They could not venture far inland because they had only a few gallons of gasoline left in the tanks and, being equipped with pontoons, could land only on water.

When a small coastal town came into view, Stultz decided to set the plane down. The fuel supply was so low that the engines were kept going only by keeping the plane level in flight. Stultz made a perfect landing out in the Channel and taxied up to a large buoy. Gordon leaped out on a pontoon and tied up to the buoy to keep the swift-running tide from carrying the *Friend-ship* farther out in the Channel. "Then, having crossed the Atlantic by air, we waited for the village to come out and welcome us."

And a cool Celtic welcome it was. Three men working on a railway line on the shore closest to them hardly looked up from their labors. It was almost half an hour before a police launch came out, and the local cop demanded to know who they were and what they were doing in the harbor. He did inform them that, in just twenty hours and forty minutes, they had flown from Trespassey Bay, Newfoundland, to Burry Port, Wales, a few miles east of Swansea, and agreed to send out a boat which would haul them to a mooring for the night. But it was more than two hours before the citizens ashore bestirred themselves and towed the *Friendship* to her overnight mooring, and Amelia and her companions jumped gratefully ashore.

8
Instant Celebrity

I_T was slow in gathering force, but once the word got around the little Welsh port that they were transatlantic fliers a roaring welcome was organized ashore. Before they left the *Friendship*, however, Hilton Railey had chartered an old Imperial Airways flying boat and flown up to Burry Port. Railey and his pilot landed a few hundred yards from Amelia's plane, and he caught sight of her "seated Indian fashion in the doorway of the fuselage and with Indian composure indifferent to the clamor ashore." Her attitude was anything but triumphant when Railey pulled up in a dory.

"Congratulations!" Railey shouted. "How does it feel to be the first woman to fly the Atlantic?"

"Hello," was all she had to say for herself.

Railey noted that they were all dead weary but that there was something in her attitude besides the inevitable letdown.

"What's the matter?" he asked, sitting next to her in the doorway. "Aren't you excited?"

"Excited?" she said listlessly. "No. It was a grand experience, but all I did was lie on my tummy and take pictures of the clouds. We didn't see much of the ocean. Bill did all the flying —had to. I was just baggage, like a sack of potatoes."

"What of it? You're still the first woman to fly the Atlantic and what's more the first woman pilot."

"Oh, well," she replied with a philosophical smile, "maybe someday I'll try it alone."

A short time later they went ashore to that dilatory Burry Port welcome. They didn't sit down to dinner that night until almost ten o'clock "after the rigors of a welcome at the hands of 10,000 enthusiastic Welshmen, disciplined by three flustered policemen." *

The official welcome, with a committee headed by Mrs. Frederick Guest and the Lady Mayor, awaited them in Southampton. Even then—with the strain of the preparations for the flight, the delays, and the flight itself—Amelia had not prepared herself for the process of instant celebrity into which she would shortly be hurled. As George Putnam would analyze it, her unpreparedness for the shock of fame was explicable because of the "enormous nervous and mental concentration of carrying the project through," so that "the human organism simply has nothing left with which to imagine outcomes." Certainly she was not outfitted for stately public receptions. Her entire baggage on arrival in Burry Port consisted, she said, of "two scarfs, a toothbrush and a comb. One scarf was quickly snatched by some enthusiast. The other stayed with me because it happened to be tied on. The toothbrush and comb also survived, probably because they were hidden in the community dufflebag, shared by Stultz, Gordon and me."

After a few hours' sleep at the Ashburnham Hotel, they returned to the *Friendship* with Hilton Railey and a reporter from the *Times* of London, who had arrived in Burry Port during the night. They all climbed aboard for the flight to Southampton, during which Stultz allowed Amelia to take the controls.

* Burry Port later erected an 18-foot monument to Amelia Earhart and her companions, saluting her as "the first woman to fly over the Atlantic Ocean."

Mrs. Guest and the Lady Mayor of Southampton, Mrs. Foster Welch, her bosom emblazoned with the gold insignia of her office, headed the civic reception for the fliers. They were then taken on a Rolls-Royce tour of the port, with the sidewalks lined by applauding Britons. Amelia was handed a cable of congratulations from President Coolidge which seemed to her to imply that the flight was her personal achievement. But she was too honest and forthright to let an undeserved compliment stand without being corrected, particularly since the credit belonged to a man who had surmounted personal and technical problems of almost frightful proportions. In her cabled reply she crisply informed the President:

SUCCESS ENTIRELY DUE GREAT SKILL OF MR. STULTZ STOP HE WAS ONLY ONE MILE OFF COURSE AT VALENTIA AFTER FLYING BLIND FOR TWO THOUSAND TWO HUNDRED FORTY-SIX MILES AT AVERAGE SPEED ONE HUNDRED AND THIRTEEN M.P.H.

Still wearing her flying suit, Amelia, with her flight companions, was borne off to London in a yellow Rolls. There she was to be the guest of Mrs. Guest for two weeks in the latter's Park Lane mansion.

From then on she was the center of a whirl of congratulation and adulation, particularly, of course, from English womanhood. From the masculine sector there was occasional sniping; the English male was more reluctant than the American to recognize that women had acquired certain inalienable rights in the past generation. The *Church Times* of London was rather huffy about the whole venture. After congratulating her on surviving the journey, it remarked: "The voyage itself, for nearly all the way through fog, is a remarkable achievement made possible by the skill and courage of the pilot. But his anxiety must have been vastly increased by the fact that he was carrying a woman passenger, and as the *Evening Standard* has properly pointed out, her presence added no more to the achievement than if the passenger had been a sheep. Miss Earhart has been acclaimed by Welsh villagers, congratulated by Mr. Coolidge, lionized in London, and she is offered large sums to appear in the films. For us, it is all a rather pitiful commentary on 'so-called civilization.' Society cannot profit directly or indirectly from Miss Earhart's journey. She is an international heroine simply and solely because, owing to good luck and an airman's efficiency, she is the first woman to travel from America to Europe by air. A scientist has died after many years of agony, because of his devotion to the work of healing, and for him there are only brief paragraphs in the newspapers, while Miss Earhart has columns. Women suffer constant discomfort and risk infection from loathsome diseases, working for the unhappy in slums, in leper colonies, in the fetid tropics, and their names remain unknown. Certainly, the sense of values in the modern world is sadly distorted."

Amelia would probably have agreed with that sermonette, would even have expressed the same ideas in stronger language. After all, until a few weeks before, she too had been "working for the unhappy in the slums" herself, and in total obscurity. But neither she nor the *Church Times'* editorial writer would be taking into account the incalculable lift such accomplishments gave the human spirit.

Even farther off the mark was the *English Review,* which snorted that transatlantic flights like those of the *Friendship* and Lindbergh's *Spirit of St. Louis* had nothing to do with the progress of aviation, that nothing could change the fact that "air transport is the most unreliable and the most expensive form of transport." Peering astigmatically into the future, and sounding much like an American editorial writer forty-odd years later complaining of the cost of the Apollo moonshot program, the *English Review* declared: "No amount of Atlantic flights will alter these facts, because they happen, as things are, to be inherent in the nature of men and things. Absurd parallels are drawn between people who talk sense about the air today, and people who preferred stagecoaches to railways. The only parallel would be, of course, between such people and any who insist today in flying to Paris by balloon instead of by aeroplane. . . . Not a single aeroplane would be flying commercially today without the Government subsidy, for the simple reason that by comparison with other forms of transport air transport is uneconomic. To talk vaguely of great developments which will occur in the future is no answer, unless you can show that the defects of air transport are technical defects which can be overcome by mechanical means."

On reading that, Amelia's only comment was that "its viewpoint is reminiscent of that when the Wrights were experimenting at Kitty Hawk." Commercial transatlantic flights were, of course, made feasible through the conquest of "technical" problems as well as the pioneering of the Lindberghs and Earharts.

Aside from such sobersided and negative reflections, England gave Amelia a wholehearted welcome. Her two weeks there, she said later, were "a jumble of teas, theatres, speech making, exhibition tennis, polo and Parliament." The *Friendship* trio were guests of honor at a dinner given by the Air League of the British Empire. But Amelia was sincerely discomfited by the fact that she was the star attraction—though it was part of the flight plan that she was to be the focus of attention—and her male colleagues were largely ignored by the spotlight.

The astringently outspoken, American-born Lady Astor invited her to Cliveden, the Astor estate, and took her to Toynbee Hall, a London settlement house, declaring, "I'm not interested in you a bit because you crossed the Atlantic by air. I want to hear about your settlement work."

She was the guest at a luncheon at the United States Embassy given by the ambassador's wife. Lord Lonsdale took her to see the Olympia Horse Show. The Prince of Wales, later Edward VIII and still later the Duke of Windsor, spotted her at a nightclub and insisted on dance after dance with her; his interest was more, or less, than romantic, since he was a pilot himself and wistfully complained, "I like to fly solo myself, but they won't let me."

Captain Railey, as her official buffer, reported that she conducted herself with unfaltering ease and grace, whether "laying
a wreath at the Cenotaph or before the statue of Edith Cavell;
whether sipping tea with the Prime Minister and Lady Astor at
the House of Commons, or talking with Winston Churchill.
. . . She remained herself, serious, forthright, with no bunk in
her makeup. Even in those days I sensed that for all her lack of
ostentation she would yet write drama in the skies: her simplic-
ity would capture people everywhere; her strength of character
would hold her on her course; in calm pursuit of an end not
personal she would achieve greatness. To me, in fact, she
seemed that she had been born with it."

The only social misstep of the English triumph, in fact, was
committed by Railey himself. Invited to Cliveden, he wore a
morning coat and silk hat, only to find Lady Astor and all the
other guests dressed in slacks or sports dresses. Railey skulked
in the library the rest of the day, explaining that "before the
afternoon's over I'll undoubtedly be taken for the butler."

Only once did Amelia manage to play hooky from the social
and official engagements made for her by the flight's backers.
The person she was most eager to meet in England was Lady
Heath, a sportswoman who had flown solo from Capetown to
London. She finally achieved that meeting and in addition obtained Lady Heath's promise to give her the use of her plane
for a few hours' recreation away from the crowds, the banquet
tables, and the inexorable lionizers.

At 5:30 one morning she slipped out of Mrs. Guest's house in
Park Lane without telling anyone where she was going. She
found a taxi rank around the corner and was driven out to the
Croydon airdrome, where Lady Heath kept her Avian Moth.
For two hours, alone at the controls, she flew through the morning skies, happy to be in her proper element. She was so delighted by the way the Moth handled that she made arrangements to buy the plane from Lady Heath before returning to
the States.

There were a few more days of being lionized, a lunch given

by American correspondents, attendance at a tattoo at Aldershot with pageantry supplied by the British air and ground forces, and then she and her coheroes sailed for the United States aboard the liner *Roosevelt*. Another, and noisier, reception awaited them in New York, and several times Amelia wistfully asked Captain Harry Manning, "Can't you take us to South America instead?"

Her contract, however, called for submission to civic welcomes in New York, Boston, and across the country. "Riding up Main Street while people throw telephone books at you," she later reflected, "is an amusing modern version of a triumphal march."

But she had more to worry about than getting conked by a telephone directory. Bill Stultz had taken to the bottle again, had brought a case of brandy aboard the *Roosevelt* and lost no time in consuming it. His $20,000 in prize money was no consolation for the deep melancholy which only flying alleviated. "Drunkenness is the only true form of happiness," he told Amelia one day after she'd found him passed out in his cabin. (Only a year later, he would find the final escape of many of his breed, death in a plane crash at Roosevelt Field, near New York.) Amelia naturally was concerned about the possibility that he might disgrace himself in public when they reached New York.

And to Captain Railey, who accompanied them on the *Roosevelt,* she confided another anxiety: that essentially she was being a phony in accepting all the adoration when "all I contributed was to lie on the floor of the fuselage like a sack of potatoes and admire the lovely clouds we were flying over." That instant celebrity could be a trap was to be demonstrated shortly, particularly the way it placed the subject in false positions. She felt it necessary to help Commander Byrd's coming venture as he had helped the *Friendship* flight. The result of her gesture was encapsulated by one of The *New Yorker*'s biting "Talk of the Town" paragraphs: "One of the greatest personal sacrifices of all times, as we look at it, was the sacrifice Miss

Earhart made in endorsing a brand of cigarettes so she could earn fifteen hundred dollars to contribute to Commander Byrd's South Pole flight. She admitted in her letter that she 'made the endorsement deliberately.' Commander Byrd, replying, said it seemed to him 'an act of astonishing generosity.' Pioneering must go on, whatever the toll; the waste places must be conquered. Since, however, the faculty of Reed University, in Oregon, declares that it is impossible for a person blindfolded to tell one cigarette from another, it seems to us the only honorable course left to Commander Byrd, in order to vindicate science and validate Miss Earhart's gift, is to fly the South Pole blindfolded."

She told Railey that the only way she could live with herself in the future would be to fly the Atlantic alone. "I'm a false heroine," she explained, "and that makes me feel guilty. Someday I will redeem my self-respect. I can't live without it."

America was still crazy over transatlantic fliers and reserved her most tumultuous welcomes for them, starting with the ritual perfected by New York City, silk-hatted Mayor Jimmy Walker greeting the trio with wisecracks and a key to the city, immersion in confetti coming up Broadway in an open car, promoters and lion-hunters swarming over them. Out of the thirty-two cities which demanded the honor of receiving them, Amelia and her companions chose New York, Boston, and Chicago. In Chicago Bill Stultz disappeared, and George Putnam, not unwillingly, put on goggles and a leather jacket and took Stultz's place beside Amelia.

Putnam, in fact, was slowly taking over her life by making himself indispensable. Unofficially he acted as her manager and advised her on endorsing commercial products, lecture offers, film contracts (all rejected), pleas for articles from newspapers and magazines. Within a few months after returning to America, she had received $50,000 from various sources, mostly advertisers, and had made herself financially independent.

The aggressive Putnam, having aced himself in as Amelia's

closest adviser, naturally became her publisher. She went into seclusion at Putnam's home in suburban Rye, New York, to write the book about the *Friendship* flight, *20 Hrs. 40 Min.*, in a matter of weeks. Her hostess was Putnam's third wife, Dorothy Binney Putnam, an attractive, intelligent, and generous-spirited woman whom Amelia—ironically, in view of future developments—liked so well that she dedicated the book to her.

After finishing the book and reading the proofs, she felt an intense desire to "get away from it all," reassert herself as an individual, free herself from public demands, and think about her future. She had already decided against returning to Denison House because somehow fame and social work didn't go together. "For the moment," she said, "all I wished to do in the world was to be a vagabond—in the air."

The swift, maneuverable little Avian she had bought from Lady Heath in England had arrived, and she decided to take off alone on a series of hops across the country to the Pacific Coast. Incidentally, it would be the first time a woman had ever flown from the Atlantic to the Pacific and back again. In 1928 flying across the country was still difficult. One small town looked pretty much like another, there were few airports, and the transcontinental pilot had to rely on landmarks, railways, rivers, and other features of the terrain. On what she called her "air-gypsying" flight across the country, she was surprised by the lack of navigational aids for the airman. "Imagine automobiling without signs! Imagine trying to recognize a new town, the way flyers do—a hundred-mile-an-hour look at a checkerboard of streets and roofs, trees and fields, with highways and railroads radiating and crisscrossing and perhaps a river or two to complicate—or simplify—the geography lesson."

America from the air was *terra incognita.* In her memoir *The Fun of It All,* she set down a transcontinental pilot's bewildered musings: "My compass reads due west. I have been flying for more than an hour. Speed 100 m.p.h. In half an hour, if the course is correct and I have allowed properly for winds, I ought to cross a river which is fifty miles from Bugville. Beyond that river is a railroad track. The first town which appears to the left should be Prune City."

Nor were the airports all they should have been. Landing at Rogers Field near Pittsburgh, the airstrip was grass-covered. She made a neat three-point landing, but then the Avian struck a shallow ditch concealed by grass and almost flipped over. The propeller was cracked, and Amelia had to lay over in Pittsburgh while spare parts were flown out from New York. She was so irritated by the accident, and by newspaper headlines claiming she had been seriously injured, that she refused to "blow a kiss at Pittsburgh" for the newspaper photographers.

She made Fort Worth safely in a series of flights, but negotiating Texas, with its vast plains and empty horizons, was almost like flying the Atlantic. Soon after leaving Fort Worth she was thrown off course when she and the Avian were shaken up and bounced around by air pockets. Worse yet, her map, which had been fastened to her shirt with a safety pin, had been blown out of the cockpit.

She kept on flying what she hoped was the right course westward until she came to a highway, which she followed into New Mexico. Her gas supply was getting low, and the sun was setting. There were plenty of automobiles on the highway below but only an occasional lonely ranch house or oil derrick to indicate the country had been settled. It was getting dark and her tanks were almost empty when she sighted a small town ahead; Hobbs, New Mexico, as she was to learn shortly. The only feasible landing place was the main street, which fortunately was empty of traffic at the dinner hour. "At high altitude where the air is thin," she later recounted, "it is necessary to make a pretty fast landing, so I am afraid I broke speed ordinances as the Avian rolled smartly through the heart of the city." Hobbs was an oil boom town just six months old when Amelia Earhart dropped out of the darkling sky. "The citizens helped me fold the wings and then, after sending telegrams by way of the single telephone, I dined at the Owl Cafe, from the much appreciated but invariable menu of fried eggs, coffee and bread. And the luxury of a real bed!"

Amelia was way off her intended course and next morning started back for Texas and her scheduled destination, El Paso. Once again she got lost and this time came down at Pecos, Texas, with one of the tires on her landing wheels flat from a thorn puncture. The natives not only repaired her tire but carried her off to a Rotary luncheon. Taking off for El Paso that afternoon, the Avian developed engine trouble, and Amelia had to make a forced landing in the mesquite. Once again luck was with her. She had come down near a highway, and a number of motorists soon sped to her assistance. The plane was towed back to Pecos and a three-day layover waiting for spare parts to arrive from El Paso.

She made it to Los Angeles in time to watch the start of the National Air Races, then flew back East with only a few minor mishaps to mar the journey.

On her return to New York early in the autumn of 1928, Amelia found that George Putnam, as her agent, had lined up more lecture engagements than she could have fulfilled and also had received offers from *McCall's* and *Cosmopolitan* magazines for her to join their staffs. Subsequently *McCall's* withdrew its offer because it did not carry cigarette advertising and Amelia had been endorsing certain brands. That still left *Cosmopolitan*, then edited by the brilliant but erratic Ray Long. For the next year Amelia turned out an article almost every month for *Cosmopolitan* on subjects that interested her, all of them dealing with aviation. In accepting that offer, she said, "I knew that I was casting my lot permanently with aviation." Thus she reached the *Cosmopolitan* audience with such themes as "Try Flying Yourself"; "How Fanny Hurst Could Learn to Fly," Miss Hurst being a *Cosmopolitan* author; "Is It Safe for You to Fly?"; "Shall You Let Your Daughter Fly?"; "Why Are Women Afraid to Fly?" She was also kept busy answering the hundreds of letters she received as aviation editor of the magazine. Oddly, many of her correspondents were eager to learn just how well she knew Lindbergh; others wanted her autograph or asked such questions as why a monoplane was faster than a biplane.

Eventually, perhaps inevitably, Amelia found the work too confining. Also, in the back of her mind there was the idea of vindicating herself for the "false" fame, as she regarded it, which she had acquired on the *Friendship* flight. For the next several years much of her life was filled with preparations aimed in the general direction of eventually flying the Atlantic by herself.

Early in 1929 it was announced that the first Women's Air Derby—journalistically retitled the "powder puff derby"— would be held that August. Amelia promptly sold her lightweight Avian and bought a Lockheed Vega, which was more powerful, a high-wing monoplane capable of longer and faster flights. From now on, her life would be devoted more to flying than to lecturing, editing, writing, or posing for photographers.

9
Angels, Skylarks, and Birdwomen

ON a Sunday afternoon, August 18, 1929, twenty planes piloted by women lined up in two rows on the runway of Clover Field near Santa Monica, California, for the first Women's Air Derby. It was regarded as the first serious test of feminine flying capabilities under the stress of competition. All twenty of the contestants, including Amelia in her Lockheed Vega, saw the cross-country race as a critical challenge. Under the headline WOMEN'S DERBY SHOULD BE TERMINATED, one of the Los Angeles newspapers stated that challenge: "Women have been dependent on men for guidance for so long that when they are put on their own resources they are handicapped."

The contestants were outraged by that and other slurs; they saw the race (as Louise Thaden said) as "more important than life or death." Editorial gibes were answered by the Race Committee: "We wish officially to thumb our noses at the press."

Thirteen of the planes were entered in the heavier and more powerful-engined class, including Amelia's, and the others competed in the light-plane class. Amelia's rivals included Marvel Crosson, Florence (Pancho) Barnes, Blanche Noyes, Louise Thaden, Mary von Mach, Phoebe Omlie, Margaret Perry, Ruth Nichols, Opal Kunz, Mrs. Keith Miller, Claire Fahey, Thea Rasche, Ruth Elder, May Haizlip, Bobbie Trout, Gladys O'Donnell, Edith Foltz, Neva Paris, and Vera Dawn Walker.

Several of the contestants were already friends of hers, particularly Ruth Nichols (her peer as a pilot and her equal in fame), Louise Thaden, and Blanche Noyes. For the most part the rivalry was much better natured than in other forms of female competition. There was an atmosphere of comradeship, of shared dangers, known to few American women.

Ruth Nichols, and most of the others, would avow that winning wasn't the main thing. "That Amelia always seemed to manage to beat me to the starting line in record flights," she wrote in *Wings for Life,* "was simply the fall of the cards. I felt then, and I feel now that the achievements of any flyer, man or woman, advance the science and understanding of aviation, and so are of eventual benefit to all civilization."

On the other hand, the winners in such competitions could count on a fat income from advertising endorsements and other goodies. The girls did fly to win. Thea Rasche, for instance, received a telegram just before the race started which warned her BEWARE OF SABOTAGE and which was regarded as an attempt to psych her out of doing her best.

The famous film and stage comedian Will Rogers, an aviation enthusiast who was to lose his life in an Alaskan crackup with Wiley Post some years later, jestingly presided over the ceremonies at the start of the race from Santa Monica to Cleveland, referring to the entrants as ladybirds, sweethearts of the air, flying flappers, and other heavily masculine witticisms not entirely appreciated by the contingent of leather-jacketed ladies waiting in their cockpits.

One by one, at one-minute intervals, the score of contestants took off at a wave of the starter's flag. The race to Cleveland was to take eight days, with prearranged stops each day and no night flying permitted. The first overnight stop was at San Bernardino, California, which all but one of the entrants made.

Amelia herself almost became a dropout the next day while crossing the desert to Yuma, Arizona. On landing at Yuma she ran into a sandbank and damaged her propeller. The other contestants sportingly voted to extend the layover in Yuma to three hours while the damage to Amelia's plane was repaired.

At some of the stops there were banquets; at others they were lucky to find restrooms in working order. The male speakers at some of the festivities along the way insisted on referring to the contestants as angels or ladybirds, aping Will Rogers, and the race itself as a lipstick or powderpuff or petticoat derby. Amelia would smile bravely or grimly at such remarks, then advise the male banqueters that they were to be called fliers or pilots, that they had earned the right to equal dignity with male aviators.

There were accidents along the way—one of them fatal. Marvel Crosson, as her rivals learned in Fort Worth, had crashed in the Gila River country south of Phoenix. Her body was found near the wreckage with her parachute unopened. "More good pilots," the surviving contestants reassured each other, "have been killed in automobiles than will ever be killed by airplanes." Pancho Barnes stripped off her landing gear and clipped the top off a car parked too close to the airstrip at Pecos, Texas. Blanche Noyes also suffered a mishap when her plane ground-looped on landing, but neither she nor Pancho Barnes was injured.

On that same leg of the race over Texas, Ruth Elder had to find a convenient pasture because there was no ladies' room on her plane. As she later told the story to Amelia, "Pretty soon I saw a nice big pasture close by a farmhouse. There were a lot of animals in it but that didn't bother me until after I had landed, when out of a clear sky I remembered my ship is painted a brilliant red! It was too late to take off. All those creatures were jogging toward me."

"What did you do?" she was asked.

"I prayed. 'Dear God,' I prayed, 'let them all be cows!' "

There was considerable dismay at all the stops they were required to make as they hedgehopped across the country. "Claremore, Oklahoma, has grabbed off another distinction," Will Rogers wrote in his column, "it being the only town that the race officials didn't make those poor girls stop at. They've had to land in every buffalo wallow that had a Chamber of Commerce and put up a hotdog stand."

On the seventh day the surviving contestants reached Columbus, Ohio. Amelia and Ruth Nichols were leading the field in elapsed time, and their rivalry would be decided by who made the best time on the last hop into Cleveland. Next morning they lined up on the runway for the starter's signal. Taking off just ahead of Amelia, Miss Nichols' plane suddenly dipped its wing and crashed into a tractor parked at the end of the runway. The plane flipped over.

Instead of taking off in her turn and probably gaining an undisputed lead over the other contestants, Amelia immediately climbed out of the cockpit of her Lockheed and ran over to the wreckage of Miss Nichols' plane to haul her rival out. Miss Nichols was unhurt. Amelia then took off for Cleveland and the finish line but by then had lost her edge over the others. She finished in third place, behind Louise Thaden and Gladys O'Donnell.

Camaraderie had developed among the women who flew in that first race, though newspaper columnists had jokingly declared they would be pulling one another's hair out and stabbing each other with hatpins. Quite the contrary. Except for the engine-tampering charge, and in spite of the fact they were contesting for a first prize of $2,500 plus a new automobile, all the entrants had conducted themselves with the sportsmanship of an English foxhunt.

Amelia and Ruth Nichols agreed that now was the time to press their long-discussed plans for a women's flying organization. They were supported by a half-dozen members of the women's department at Curtiss Wright, including Neva Paris,

Frances Harrell, Margery Brown, Fay Gillis, Betty Huyler, and Opal Kunz—all of them fliers. There were then one hundred women in the United States who were licensed pilots.

The first organizational meeting was held November 2, 1929, at the Curtiss airport near Valley Stream on Long Island. The first subject for debate was a title for the organization. Amelia didn't make any suggestions at first but listened with quiet distress at some of the giddier offerings—Lady Birds, Gadflies, Homing Pigeons, Lady Buzzards (!), Moon Calves, Climbing Vines, Sky Scrapers, Angels' Club, Spinners, Bird Women, Breezy Birds, Queens High, and Air Dames.

After much spirited discussion, Amelia sideslipped in with her own suggestion: why not a number instead of a name, the number to be that of the charter members? There were ninety-nine original members, so the organization, it was finally decided, would be called the Ninety-Nines. At a later meeting Amelia was elected the first president, with Louise Thaden as national secretary.

Amelia was kept occupied that fall on the lecture circuit, spreading the gospel of the air age. One appearance was scheduled for Atchison, where she dedicated the new high school stadium named for her. She also finished the last articles due under her contract with *Cosmopolitan*. Not much of her sizable income stayed long in her bank account. Her father had married a fellow Christian Scientist and was worried about the mortgage payments on a house he had bought in the Los Angeles suburb of Eagle Rock. Amelia paid off the mortgage.

But Edwin Earhart did not long enjoy that cottage in the arid foothills of Los Angeles. Only a few months after the mortgage had been torn up, he learned that he had cancer of the throat. The disease was in its terminal stage, and his struggle against death was agonizing but mercifully brief. Amelia was at his bedside when he died, reflecting on how that essentially lovable, always hopeful man (like David Copperfield's friend Mr. Micawber) had lucked out on everything from the summer night he fell in love with the daughter of a house on Quality Hill. She wired her sister: DAD'S LAST BIG CASE SETTLED OUT OF COURT, PEACEFULLY AND WITHOUT PAIN.

Perhaps as an unofficial memorial to her father's victory over the same enemy, she paid for six month's sanitarium care for the husband of one of the Ninety-Nines when his alcoholism got out of control. She also helped an airplane mechanic whom she had known during her early flying days around Los Angeles buy a date ranch, and she contributed considerable sums to Denison House, of which she was a member of the board of directors.

In aviation her overriding concern now was the development of the first passenger airlines making scheduled flights. She joined Transcontinental Air Transport, the corporate parent of Transcontinental and Western and of the present Trans World Airlines, as an adviser more or less in charge of persuading women it was safe to board an airliner. Some pioneering market analysts discovered that the public's reluctance to use air transport evidently was grounded on feminine prejudice against the untried. More men would have been willing to cut their travel time, especially business executives, but were prevented from flying by their wives' fears.

TAT's operating heads were Gene Vidal and Paul Collins, both aviation veterans, but it soon became known as the "Lindbergh Line" because Colonel Lindbergh had accepted the position of chairman of its technical committee in exchange for a quarter of a million dollars in TAT stock. (There was no such inducement for Amelia Earhart as a lower-ranking celebrity.) Lindbergh's fame, it was hoped, would lure passengers. His forte, however, was not public relations, as TAT soon learned. While making survey flights for the new airline, he landed one day in May, 1928, at the Amarillo, Texas, airport and displayed what the newspapers called an "angry annoyance" at a crowd of the curious who gathered around him. The result was a minor tempest of bad publicity for TAT just when it was struggling to get off the ground. Gene Howe, the brother of the editor of Amelia's hometown paper, was the editor of the Amarillo *News-Globe* and nationally celebrated for his column "The Tactless Texan." Regarding the airport incident, he wrote that "Lindbergh is only a boy, still moist behind the ears, and even if he has flown to Paris there is no reason why he should be permitted to be discourteous to those who have a natural and wholesome impulse to see him." Howe himself was counterattacked by his journalistic colleagues as "a cheap publicity adventurer who has attacked a public idol for the purpose of attracting attention." It wasn't exactly the kind of publicity TAT could use in promoting air travel with the help of the Lindbergh name. Amelia observed the fuss at a distance and resolved never to lose her own temper with those faceless but still human crowds which yearned for contact with the famous and notorious.

Her own work for TAT was more obscure but just as vital to the company's prospects. She not only flew a number of TAT's routes but took charge of the traffic department and tried to iron out its difficulties with maintaining flight schedules.

She was determined that in the near future American travelers would accept airlines as a necessity rather than an exotic adventure. "Airplanes," she noted, "sometimes offered no advantages over ground facilities in time saving, if they didn't fly often enough to be a convenience to passengers.

"For instance, a man who wished, say, to go to Cleveland from New York might find a plane left for the west once a day at nine o'clock in the morning. If he couldn't leave until noon, he would make better time by taking a train that night and arriving at Cleveland about the time the next plane was leaving from New York. But the operators couldn't be expected to put on a heavy schedule to accommodate only a few customers. To reach enough to justify several additional trips a day, it was obvious fares would have to be reduced."

Amelia kept a close watch on how ticket sellers handled women passengers, coaching them on how to allay feminine fears, and encouraged the plane crews to explain all about air pockets, cabin temperatures, and the change in pressure which often caused piercing earaches.

It was easy working with the two founders of TAT because both had been working pilots themselves, Vidal with the Army Air Corps, Collins as a veteran airmail pilot with eight thousand hours logged. She used the line to get around the country and fill speaking engagements, often taking her mother with her. "To her," Amelia said, "flying became so commonplace that she took along a detective story to keep awake when we were in the air for long periods." When someone in her lecture audience would question her about the perils of flying as a passenger, she would point to her mother, seated nearby on the platform, as an example of a woman who had easily outgrown her fears of air travel.

Amelia became more closely involved with airline operations in 1930 when Vidal and Collins, supported by Philadelphia investors, decided to establish the New York, Philadelphia and Washington Airway with an hourly service (ten round trips daily) between New York and the other two cities. She was named vice-president of what she called the "first really frequent service in the world." Outside experts scorned the idea, declaring no airline could survive without a government subsidy or mail contracts, but in its first year the Airway carried 66,279 passengers and its planes flew 1,523,400 miles.

As vice-president, Amelia's duties were mainly those of a propagandist. "There were endless letters to be answered, and many many speeches to audiences of various kinds. Always my talks were about flying from one point of view or another. During this period of vocal salesmanship, I met college girls, women's clubs, professional groups and mixtures of these, as well as all sorts and conditions of men before whom I also spoke."

When she wasn't propagandizing on behalf of air travel, she was roving up and down the line, checking on passengers' comfort on the ten-seat planes, listening to and straightening out complaints in the terminals. Once she chaperoned a canary belonging to a VIP from New York to Washington. The Airway had adopted a liberal policy toward taking animals on its flights. It even sold two seats to a pony, though the animal had to stand with its rump partly in the aisle.

Busy as she was with executive responsibilities, Amelia found time to widen her experience as a pilot. She set new speed records for women over 1-mile and 100-kilometer courses and began flying an autogiro, the early model of the helicopter, in which she set an altitude record of 18,415 feet.

All that was merely on the fringes of her main ambition to fly the Atlantic solo. To emulate Lindbergh and become the first woman to make that flight she needed all the piloting experience she could get, particularly over long distances, plus navigational instruction, plus some knowledge of meteorology. For the last, she went to Dr. James H. Kimball, chief meteorologist of the New York Weather Bureau, and unofficially became his pupil. She spent hours standing beside his countinghouse desk in the Weather Bureau on top of the Whitehall Building in lower Manhattan, watching while he read telegraph flimsies containing reports from land stations and ships at sea, then drew weather maps with wavy lines representing isobars, isotherms, high and low pressure areas. From Dr. Kimball, a courtly, middle-aged Southerner, she learned that storm systems generally move from west to east over the United States, that the prevailing winds over the Atlantic are westerly. She also learned that storm centers revolve in a counterclockwise fashion when north of the equator. All this was exceedingly valuable to a young woman whose aerial ambitions ranged the world. Dr. Kimball was an endlessly patient instructor because he believed that such flights such as hers pioneered a regular transocean air service, which was being held up, in his opinion, only because there wasn't enough accurate weather information available. Another inhibiting factor, of particular interest to Amelia, was the enormous size of North Atlantic storms, which often extend from Newfoundland to Britain.

Two years after the *Friendship* flight, three years after his own, Colonel Lindbergh was still the model, the prototype, whom Amelia looked up to with something close to hero worship.

She had become friendly with Lindbergh and his wife, the former Anne Morrow, when TAT inaugurated its coast-to-coast passenger service (forty-eight hours with frequent stopovers). Lindbergh piloted one of the inaugural flights to Los Angeles, on which Amelia and Mrs. Lindbergh were passengers. The latter had learned to fly, and Amelia admired her almost as much as her husband. "With her diminutive figure engulfed in ungainly [flying] togs, she looks like a tiny teddy bear beside her six-foot-something husband," Amelia observed.

On the return flight Amelia and her secretary took thirteen pieces of luggage between them. Lindbergh had always admonished his wife to keep luggage to the bare minimum. When he caught sight of the mound of luggage brought by Amelia and her companion, Lindbergh turned to his wife and said, "Don't you get any foolish ideas from this."

Amelia considered the Lindberghs' an ideal marriage, not only because of its romantic aspects, but because they were both fliers and on a flight to the Orient Mrs. Lindbergh had acted as her husband's navigator and radio operator. It seemed to her that the couple shared more of their lives with each other than any other she had known.

About her own matrimonial prospects she was much more dubious. Obviously her husband could be no ordinary fellow. "Marriage is a mutual responsibility," she insisted. "And I cannot see why husbands shouldn't share in the responsibility of the home." By that, she added, she meant "something more detailed" than merely "keep a roof over the collective head and coal in the furnace." A willing and persistent suitor, though unfortunately still married, had been waiting to make Amelia his bride, even under such feminist conditions, ever since the *Friendship* flight.

10
The Bride Wore Brown

*T*HE man who marries a celebrity and intends to be a husband as well as a luggage-bearing consort requires a resilient ego and a large amount of self-confidence. It helps considerably if he is successful in his own right. Even more if he is a man of affairs able and willing to spare the time to manage his wife's career.

George Palmer Putnam figured that he fulfilled the requirements. He was a hard-driving, ambitious fellow with the habit of command. Though he had inherited his position in the publishing industry, to some extent, he would have been a success in any case. Rimless glasses may have given him the appearance of a sedate professor of history, but he was a man of action who possessed a strongly competitive urge and hated to lose out in anything, whether it was a business deal or a woman. He had attended Harvard and the University of California at Berkeley, cut himself loose from his wealthy family with $300 in his pocket, and announced his determination to achieve success on his own. Within a few years he was not only the editor of the local newspaper but mayor of Bend, Oregon. After World War I he took over the family firm of G. P. Putnam's Sons, one of the oldest publishing houses in America, and revitalized it by publishing the early works of Alexander Woollcott, Ben Hecht, and Edward Streeter, as well as a whole array of first-person accounts by the period's leading explorers and adventurers.

By his own account he had proposed to Amelia six times between 1928 and late 1930 and had been turned down. Amelia was wary of marriage, having been disillusioned as a child by her parents' unhappiness; furthermore, she was a feminist—as well as utterly feminine in most ways—and except for the Lindberghs', saw few happy marriages around her. She was the sort who, using up her energies in many ways, could be perfectly happy unmarried. Furthermore, her career did not lend itself to any of the ordinary restrictions and coventionalities of marriage. She was, in fact, doing beautifully on her own.

It was also true that many of her friends did not like Putnam, considered him too aggressive and hard-nosed. Amelia, however, had known enough ineffectual men, beginning with her father, not to be dismayed by that facet of his character.

Putnam and his third wife were separated in 1929 and divorced the following year, Dorothy Binney Putnam removing herself and their two young sons to Florida, where she obtained the divorce, and leaving Putnam with his large and comfortable house in Rye.

Shortly after being divorced, he proposed to Amelia in a hangar at the Lockheed aircraft factory in Burbank, California, while she was waiting for her plane to be warmed up. She listened gravely, then, to Putnam's surprise, nodded in agreement, patted him on the arm, and ran off to climb into the cockpit of her plane. Just like that. Putnam was stunned, could hardly believe she had accepted. He did not see her until several days later, upon which she confirmed the acceptance. It was typical of her to take such a step casually, quickly, and with a minimum of emotion. As she often said, she always made up her mind on the spur of the moment—and then stuck by her decision.

The news of their engagement was not joyously received by

Amelia's mother. "Mother opposed marriage," as Muriel Earhart Morrissey recalled in her memoir *Courage Is the Price,* "upon the dual grounds that GP was twelve years Amelia's senior and a divorced man. Neither of these objections had any weight with Amelia. . . ."

She was thirty-two years old and knew her own mind. Best of all, George Putnam was capable of understanding her attitude. "She wanted to owe no one anything—any more spiritually than financially," as Putnam wrote of her. "In her heart she knew too that, for good or ill, she must keep freedom in a measure which is not always possible in marriage. She had no selfish dream of the anatomy of freedom, but she did know it for an element without which she personally could not do, as some plants can do without water but cannot survive without air."

Amelia rightly believed that Putnam was mature enough, self-confident enough, and generous-spirited enough to give her the freedom she required. Yet there was a last-moment wavering the morning they were married in his mother's old house in Noank, Connecticut, on February 7, 1931.

She had appeared for the ceremony, which was to be performed by a judge who was an old friend of the Putnam family, in a bridal costume only Amelia Earhart would have considered appropriate. It consisted of a brown suit, not at all new, with a crepe blouse and brown lizardskin shoes. She was hatless, as usual.

And just before the ceremony was to take place the bride-to-be handed the prospective bridegroom a letter which might— with a less stouthearted groom—have canceled the event forthwith.* It was her declaration of independence, addressed to "GP" and signed "AE," and read:

There are some things which should be writ before we are married. Things we have talked over before—most of them.

* With equally characteristic candor, Putnam included the document, "brutal in its frankness, but beautiful in its honesty," in his biography of Amelia, *Soaring Wings* (1939).

You must know again my reluctance to marry, my feeling that I shatter thereby chances in work which means so much to me. I feel the move just now as foolish as anything I could do. I know there may be compensations, but have no heart to look ahead.

In our life together I shall not hold you to any medieval code of faithfulness to me, nor shall I consider myself bound to you similarly. If we can be honest I think the differences which arise may best be avoided.

Please let us not interfere with each other's work or play, nor let the world see private joys or disagreements. In this connection I may have to keep some place where I can go to be myself now and then, for I cannot guarantee to endure at all times the confinements of even an attractive cage.

I must exact a cruel promise, and this is that you will let me go in a year if we find no happiness together.

I will try to do my best in every way.

With all his self-assurance and his insight into her character, Putnam must have been chilled by that virtual ultimatum, but he smiled bravely and nodded in agreement, and the marriage took place. He deftly handled the reporters who swarmed around the porch of his mother's house, later commenting, "They were wasting their time expecting to find AE a sort of Craig's Wife, with her marriage and her career all nicely departmentalized in advance. So much time for marriage, so much time for flying, and the most correct theories regarding the dovetailing of each worked out by slide rule."

Far from interfering with Amelia's career, Putnam promoted it with even greater vigor than before. He sold his interest in G. P. Putnam's Sons to a cousin, Palmer C. Putnam, and became head of the editorial board of Paramount Pictures. In that job he initiated a number of film projects, including one of the earlier and more successful aviation epics, *Wings*, in which Gary Cooper made his hesitant debut. Putnam was not tied to a studio desk and had to appear on the Paramount lot mainly for conferences, which gave him plenty of time to manage and promote Amelia Earhart. They maintained homes in Hollywood, in Rye, and in New York City.

Putnam kept his new wife so busy that they had no time for a honeymoon. She was then touring the country in an autogiro which advertised Beechnut chewing gum. Occasionally they would take a break in their separate activities for a reunion in the spacious home at Rye, where they entertained fellow celebrities and had Putnam's two sons up for visits from Florida. And Amelia was particularly pleased by the fact that two women she liked and admired also lived in Rye. One was Cornelia Otis Skinner, whose acting and writing careers proved a woman could combine domesticity with professional success. Another was Ruth Nichols, with whom she was in a neck-and-neck race for the distinction of being the outstanding woman flier. "It was easy to visit each other on the spur of the moment," Miss Nichols has recalled. "We were united by a common bond of interest. We spoke each other's language— and that was the language of pioneer women of the air. . . . I suppose, after Amelia's marriage to Putnam, I may have felt a few twinges of envy that she was able always to obtain the latest and finest planes, while I had to search for backers for any flight I undertook. But I know, also, that there was no bitterness in my envy. I liked and admired her, and I believe she felt the same way about me. . . . Both Amelia and I had crackups and successes. We both won a lot and lost a lot. But we were privileged to have places in the starting lineup of our country's women flyers, and each of us fulfilled her destiny as she saw it."

The country was then sliding into a depression that lasted through the decade, but the Earhart-Putnam household—she always insisted on using her maiden name—did not suffer from its effects.

With his managerial flair and promotional genius, Putnam capitalized extensively on Amelia's fame. He literally made her not only a household word but a brand name. Her picture appeared on billboards advertising cigarettes (though, she admitted, she rarely smoked more than three a year herself). Amelia Earhart lightweight airplane luggage was an immediate success, with Amelia drawing royalties on every item sold. Her name appeared on the labels of a line of women's clothes, severely tailored suits, floppy pajamas, and coats with buttons shaped like bolts.

But occasionally she drew the line, firmly and irrevocably. She didn't mind lending her name to advertisements for the Franklin automobile with its air-cooled engine, or spending part of her time designing the sort of clothes she liked herself, but some of the propositions were a little too mercenary to be acceptable. The Amelia Earhart Friendship Flight Hat was an example. It was a drab little cloche model turned out by a children's clothing manufacturer for about fifty cents, which caused shudders up and down Seventh Avenue. With Amelia's signature reproduced on the hatband it would sell for three dollars.

Amelia examined the Friendship Flight Hat one day at a business conference at a New York hotel. She had just enough experience as a designer to know shoddy workmanship when she saw it and flung it aside.

"This," she told Putnam crisply, "won't do at all."

"But I've already signed the contract with the manufacturer," Putnam protested. "He's already got a large supply in stock."

"Then," Amelia retorted, "he can unmake them. I won't be a party to cheating kids."

There was a first-class row, Amelia threatening to sue Putnam himself if the hats were placed on the market. Putnam finally had to negotiate a cancellation of the contract. Already she was image-conscious, determined to avoid any catchpenny schemes that would cheapen her reputation. It was Hilton Railey's belief that her affairs "required precious little management," that her "own unerring instincts" were the only guidance she needed. She would "cash in" only to the point required by the financing of her career.

Railey was certain that "financial gain and personal aggrandizement were minor interests" with her. "To be sure," he observed in his memoir, "flying was Amelia's job, and anyone is entitled to make a living from his job. Amelia's flights provided new material for books, magazine articles, and the lectures which she was constantly called upon to give. Genuinely as a tribute to her sex rather than for her own glorification, she accepted the honors that accrued—for the participation of women in aviation, which at all times she strove to encourage and pace, was the obsession that lured her. . . . Of herself as a 'whoopla artist' Amelia had simple, clear-eyed, at times amused appreciation; and yet with awareness of her vulnerability in this respect she did her utmost, sincerely and unselfishly, to utilize her position for the benefit of aviation."

Aside from occasional disputes over the management of her career, according to those who knew them best, the Earhart-Putnam alliance worked smoothly. Amelia decided to take up her option on the marriage after the year's trial she had insisted upon, and that was the best evidence the marriage was working. She would not be dominated even by a man accustomed to dominating others. Both being businesslike people, they divided household expenses equally and placed surplus earnings in a joint savings account. Amelia believed that the strains of marriage were eased only when the wife could pay her own way. "The individual independence of dollars and cents tends to keep a healthy balance of power in the kingdom of the home. . . . Assistants more skilled than myself can be employed to substitute in the housewife role without robbing a marriage of its essence. . . . Thus—for me—can joyful luxuries like low-wing monoplanes be had—as adding to the sum total of contentment."

Putnam was even capable of laughing easily, though with a glint in his eye, when someone playfully or inadvertently addressed him as "Mr. Earhart."

11
Harbour Grace to Londonderry

*F*OR four years Amelia had been inwardly tormented, feeling that there was something fraudulent about her fame. She could not help wincing whenever anyone referred to her as "Lady Lindy." The title of premier woman flier of the world, she felt, had not been fairly won. It was more the product of publicity and promotion than her own accomplishments. Her career was a see-through tissue of newspaper headlines, she herself a creature of the fame-making machinery of communications.

All that time, however, she had been training herself for vindication, even if that were needed only to still her own conscience. She had logged over a thousand hours in the air. Many of those hours had been taken up by instrument flying, learning to navigate "blind" through the worst possible weather conditions. She had prepared herself in every possible way for the grueling effort of flying the Atlantic solo.

And she wanted to be the first woman to do so, even though Ruth Nichols, as usual, was breathing down her neck. Miss Nichols, in fact, had started on such a venture only the year before, in June of 1931, but her plane had cracked up on landing at St. John, New Brunswick. She had just recovered from her injuries and was getting ready to try again.

Early in the spring of 1932, Amelia and Putnam were living at his Rye house. They invited Bernt Balchen over for lunch. The Norwegian-born Balchen had long ago proved himself over polar skies, North and South; he had participated in Amundsen's dirigible flight over the North Pole in 1926, the Richard Byrd-Floyd Bennett flight over the North Pole, the Byrd expedition to the South Pole, and other far-ranging aerial adventures.

They went out on the croquet pitch behind the garden and took up the mallets under the April sunshine. The crocuses were beginning to bloom. The oaks and elms were starting to leaf. It was a beautiful early spring day.

When they reached the middle wicket, it was obvious that Amelia's mind was focused on neither the beauty of an early spring nor the game of croquet.

She laid her mallet down suddenly, impulsively, and announced that she wanted to tell Balchen something. Putnam knew what was coming; they had discussed it over the breakfast table one winter morning several months before.

She wanted to fly the Atlantic, she announced when they had seated themselves on a rocky ledge nearby. And she fired three questions at Balchen: "Am I ready to do it? Is the plane ready? Will you help me?"

Balchen was a deliberate man who knew that danger of any kind must be studied carefully. He also knew that Amelia had thought out the hazards of the proposed flight long before taking it up for discussion. The most important thing was whether *she* believed she could do it.

Balchen finally cleared his throat and said, "Yes, you can do it. The plane—when we are through with it—will be okay. And, yes, I will help."

It was agreed, in that informal conference under the April sun, that Balchen would act as technical adviser for the flight. He would supervise adjustments to her Lockheed Vega mono-

The Bloomer Girls—Muriel on the swing, Amelia on her homemade stilts.

Amelia as a Chicago high school student.

Amy and Edwin Earhart during the early years of their marriage.

Amelia in her nurse's aide uniform at Spadina Military Hospital, Toronto.

Amelia as the bobbed-hair girl graduate of the twenties.

Amelia beside her much-prized plane, the Kinner Canary.

(The photos on this and the preceding page courtesy of the Amelia Earhart Collection of the Schlesinger Library, Radcliffe College.)

Amelia Earhart greeted in England after her first flight across the Atlantic.
At the left is Lew Gordon, mechanic; to the right, Wilmer Stultz, pilot, and
the mayor of Southampton. *(Underwood & Underwood)*

Enroute to Newfoundland for her first solo transatlantic flight—Amelia and Bernt Balchen at Teterboro Airport, New Jersey, May, 1932. *(Wide World)*

Mayor James J. Walker presents New York's special medal honoring Amelia Earhart for her record transatlantic flight, June, 1932. *(Wide World)*

President Herbert Hoover presenting Amelia Earhart with the National Geographic Society's gold medal in recognition of her transatlantic flight, June, 1932. At the left is Gilbert Grosvenor, president of the National Geographic Society; at the right is Mrs. Hoover.
(Underwood & Underwood)

Charles A. Lindbergh and Amelia Earhart after receiving medals for their achievements from the Rumanian government, January, 1933. Between them is the Rumanian minister to the United States. *(Wide World)*

Amelia Earhart and Eleanor Roosevelt after their night flight over Washington in April, 1933. *(Wide World)*

George Palmer Putnam bids his wife good-bye before she takes off on her attempted globe-circling flight, June 1, 1937. *(Wide World)*

Amelia Earhart and her navigator, Fred Noonan, in Batavia, Java, during a stopover on their round-the-world flight. *(Wide World)*

LICENSE RENEWALS	
INSPECTOR'S ENDORSEMENT	EXPIRATION DATE
Locust Ave., Rye, N.Y.	
Union Air Terminal, Burbank, Calif.	
864.00	26.24	10-15-31
1000.00	128.00	4/15/
	160.00	10/15/
	125.00	4/15/
	OK ?	10/15/3
	75	4/15/

Note: All provisions lations are made a though written herein.
of the Air Commerce Regu- part of the terms hereof ap

| | 11.30 | 10/ |
| | 50.00 | 4-15-35 |

A photographic copy of Amelia Earhart's pilot's license. Note the handwritten "Lost 7/2/37" across the front of the license. *(Wide World)* plane with the Wright Whirlwind engine. He would also serve as "cover" for the flight. Amelia insisted that all the preparations and the takeoff itself, as in the *Friendship* flight, must be kept secret. Balchen and Lincoln Ellsworth were preparing for a flight to the South Pole, and as far as the world was concerned, his work on Amelia's plane could be taken as preparations for the polar expedition.

Amelia had chosen Balchen as her adviser not only because he and his wife were personal friends but because he was an expert in aircraft engineering—and it was the plane, as much as the pilot, that had to come through with the best possible performance. Also, she wrote, Balchen, like herself to a lesser extent, "has the happy characteristic of conservatism and being unhurried in his judgments. At the outset we told Bernt that if at any time he thought I couldn't do it, or the ship couldn't do it, I would quit, and no harm done. But Bernt never once wavered in his confidence, and that confidence helped immeasurably in sustaining my own."

From that April day on, preparations went forward at full tilt, with Teterboro Airport in New Jersey as their headquarters. In a hangar there Balchen and his crew of mechanics straightened out the fuselage of the Lockheed, which had been battered in various forced landings. The new supercharged 500-horsepower Wasp engine from Pratt & Whitney was installed and subjected to rigorous tests. To increase the fuel capacity extra tanks were fitted into the wings and another in the cabin, which gave the plane a cruising radius of 3,200 miles.

And there was, in those secret preparations for Amelia's solo across the Atlantic, a coincidental human link with the Apollo flights of almost four decades later. The man in charge of determining the right fuel mix at Teterboro for the hop to Newfoundland, then the jump across the Atlantic, was an Army pilot named Major Edwin Aldrin. His son would become an astronaut, a member of the Apollo crew which undertook the second voyage to the moon.

Meanwhile Amelia was taking an intensive course in meteorology under Dr. Kimball at the New York Weather Bureau and practicing blind flying whenever possible.

It was decided that Balchen would fly the plane up to Harbour Grace with a mechanic named Eddie Gorski and Amelia as passengers. Toward the middle of May Balchen and his crew had finished their work, and nothing was holding up departure but the weather. A low-pressure area with heavy clouds and rain persisted in the eastern Atlantic. All Amelia could do was chafe and wait for the go signal from Dr. Kimball.

That the departure took place on May 20, 1932—five years to the day after Lindbergh soloed to Paris—was a coincidence dictated by the happenstance of weather conditions. In any case, there weren't the prolonged delays—or the emotional wear and tear—which had preceded the *Friendship* flight. And that was largely due to Bernt Balchen's efficient management of the preparatory stages of the venture.

Everything was set by May 18, except for the storm pattern which hovered over the eastern Atlantic. On May 19 the low-pressure area still hadn't moved. On the morning of May 20, with Putnam standing by at the New York Weather Bureau, Amelia left the house in Rye and drove over to the Teterboro Airport, determined to be on hand if they got clearance from Dr. Kimball. She arrived about 11:30 A.M. and was looking over the plane when Eddie Gorski came out and announced there was a call for her on the hangar phone.

Putnam was on the line with the news that Dr. Kimball, after looking over the latest reports from land stations and ships at sea, believed the route up the northeastern coast was clear enough for the flight.

"All the way to Newfoundland?" she asked.

"At least as far as St. John's," Putnam replied, "and probably all the way to Harbour Grace. A high-pressure area is moving down on Newfoundland."

"Okay, we'll go this afternoon," Amelia said without hesitation. "I'll see Bernt and we'll take off as soon as possible."

No good-byes. Amelia didn't believe in them. After a hasty

conference with Balchen, it was decided they would take off at 3 P.M., which gave Amelia time to drive back to Rye and pick up her well-seasoned leather jacket and jodhpurs. She made it back to the airport at 2:55. Twenty minutes later, with Balchen at the controls, Gorski in the cockpit beside him, and Amelia lying on the cabin floor behind the extra fuel tank, they roared down the runway at Teterboro and headed for Canada.

Amelia slept most of the way, the flight to St. John's taking three hours and forty minutes. After an overnight stay in St. John's, they flew on to Harbour Grace, Newfoundland, the next day. A detailed weather report had been telegraphed from New York giving the go-ahead.

She had been resting at a hotel in town when the telegram from Putnam arrived. Balchen called her and in his matter-of-fact way suggested that she take off immediately for the other side of the Atlantic. Everything was done with dispatch. While she was being driven out to the airstrip, Balchen was drawing up a flight plan and Gorski was tuning up the engine.

With Nordic phlegm and precision, Balchen described her departure in his journal (as quoted in his autobiography, *Come North with Me*): "She arrives at the field in jodhpurs and leather flying jacket, her close-cropped blonde hair tousled, quiet and inobtrusive as a young Lindbergh.

"She listens calmly, only biting her lip a little, as I go over with her the course to hold, and tell her what weather she can expect on the way across the ocean.

"She looks at me with a small lonely smile and says, 'Do you think I can make it?' and I grin back: 'You bet.'

"She crawls calmly into the cockpit of the big empty airplane, starts the engine, runs it up, checks the mags, and nods her head. We pull the chocks, and she is off."

Her traveling gear was as Spartan as the manner of her takeoff. Not even a dress for the receptions which would await her if the flight was a success. The only food she brought was a Thermos bottle of soup and a can of tomato juice, punctured, with a straw inserted. "A pilot whose land plane falls into the

Atlantic"—her Lockheed was equipped with wheels rather than floats—"is not consoled by caviar sandwiches," she had reflected before the flight. "Everything but the bare essentials would distract my attention from the main object. Advance publicity—the questions of reporters, the protesting and/or congratulatory messages of friends, commercial overtures—all would have been unimportant and exhausting. Worse, they would have *committed* me to a flight I wanted to make because I wanted to, not by compulsion of advance ballyhoo—which might easily deprive me in the end of woman's inalienable right to change her mind."

She took off with sunset lingering on the lakes and tundra behind her. When the moon came up as she arrowed eastward over the calm sea, it was partly concealed by clouds. She had climbed to 12,000 feet, then leveled off for what looked like a smooth progress over the North Atlantic.

Then her luck began a turn for the worse. First it was the altimeter: The hand on the dial began swinging around; it was obviously out of commission.

And with incredible swiftness the weather turned against her. One moment she was sailing through a moonlit sky. The next, clouds were blotting out the moon. A few minutes later her plane was being buffeted by what she hoped was only a patch of storm. Instead she had to ride out almost an hour of rain and lightning. Catching a glimpse of the moon through layers of cloud, she decided to try climbing above the storm. Trouble was, she had no way of knowing just how high she was with the altimeter broken. Too high and she'd start picking up ice on the wings, which could be fatal in a day when deicing equipment had not been developed.

The feel of the plane was all wrong, the controls were sluggish, and she wasn't climbing as fast as she should.

Then she spotted the telltale sign of slush on the windshield. The tachometer, which registered the motor's revolutions per minute and told her how much power she was using, had picked up ice and started spinning the hand on the dial.

From then on, she had to fight her way every mile of the storm-tossed hours around midnight. If she were able to look out on the wings, she knew, they would be coated with ice. The only course was to fly lower and let the ice melt off. Fog at a lower altitude would forward the melting process. At the same time she knew it was dangerous, given their dubious accuracy, to trust her instruments—those still operating—and fly blind.

She brought the plane down so low, in fact, that she caught a glimpse of the waves breaking through the fog layers beneath her. Even she must have known a split second of panic. Hastily she hauled back on the controls, gunned the engine, and brought the plane up to a safer level.

As she later described that moment, which had brought her very close to the end of everything, she had gone into a spin while descending and almost lost control of the plane. "I carried a barograph, an instrument which records on a disc the course of a plane, its rate of ascent and descent, its levels of flight all coordinated with clocked time. My telltale disc could tell a tale. At one point it recorded an almost vertical drop of 3,000 feet. It started at an altitude of something over 3,000 feet, and ended—well, something above the water. That happened when the plane suddenly iced up and went into a spin. How long we spun I do not know. I do know that I tried my best to do exactly what one should do with a spinning plane, and regained flying control as the warmth of the lower altitude melted the ice. As we righted and held level again, through the blackness below I could see the whitecaps too close for comfort."

She had passed the point of no return, and there was nothing to do but press on through the heavy overcast. Trust the gyro-compass and hope it would guide her to a landfall. If the Wasp engine kept functioning, she had a fair chance of making it.

The clouds thinned somewhat as the night wore on. Occasionally she would catch a glimpse of a star. Hour after hour she crouched in the cockpit, hands gripping the controls, eyes glued to the instrument panel or peering through the windshield. Every fifteen minutes she had to set the Sperry gyro-compass to a new heading. The only food she took was the can of tomato juice, at which she sipped from time to time. Opening the thermos of soup would have been too much trouble.

Mechanically, the Lockheed functioned well. There was a flicker of alarm when she noticed flames shooting out through a crack in the exhaust manifold, but it was made of heavy metal, and she believed it would last until the flight was over. If it did splinter and break off, however, the flight would end very suddenly.

At first light she found herself flying between two layers of cloud, one above her at about 20,000 feet, the other below her and apparently hugging the surface of the sea. Ten hours had passed since takeoff. The sunlight was blinding, and she had to slip on a pair of dark glasses. Far below she glimpsed a ship, possibly an oil tanker, through the lower layer of clouds.

The exhaust manifold had begun vibrating badly, indicating it wouldn't last much longer. The nearest land, if her navigation had been fairly precise, was Ireland. If the flight had been smoother, she would have liked to land in Paris, à la Lindbergh, but that was out of the question now. The northern Irish coast was her best bet. She set the compass on a new heading, due east, because the wind most of the night had been from the northwest and might have blown her slightly off course.

An intense weariness, the result of flying from sunset to dawn, and now beyond, under the most tense and trying conditions, had taken a grip on her.

There was a humped shape, slowly assuming a sharper definition, through the haze ahead. Land. The hills of Donegal. A thunderstorm was lashing the eastern coast of Ireland, and she decided to turn north out of fear of plowing into the mountains. The gleaming line of a railroad—the pioneer aviator's best friend—ran up the coast. She followed it, hoping it would lead to a city large enough to have an airport. A city she later learned was Londonderry appeared below; she circled, looked for an airport, didn't find one, and decided to come down on the most promising of the meadows around the city.

"I succeeded in frightening all the cattle in the county, I think," she said later, "as I came down low several times before finally landing in a long, sloping meadow." It was a smooth landing. She cut the switch and locked on the brakes. Her watch told her that she had flown from Harbour Grace to Londonderry in fifteen hours and eighteen minutes—more than five hours faster than the *Friendship* flight.

A farmer came clumping over the pasture in his Wellingtons and stared open-jawed into the cockpit.

Amelia grinned and said, "I've come from America."

"Have you now?" Dan McCallion asked. His employer, Patrick Gallagher, and several dairymaids came running up to be similarly astonished. Gallagher borrowed a neighbor's car and took her to a house a half-dozen miles down the road where there was a telephone. The Irish phone service rivals the French in sheer perversity, but she managed to put through a transatlantic call to George Putnam in New York and tell him where she had landed. Then she went back to Gallagher's farm home and slept through the afternoon and night.

When she awakened that Sunday morning, she found the world outside those green Irish hills clamoring to embrace her. Paramount News had dispatched a plane to the Londonderry airport to bring her to London. Lady Astor insisted that Amelia must be her guest in St. James's Square, adding, "I will lend you a nightgown." The Lindberghs had cabled their congratulations. King George V's Minister for Air had conveyed his sovereign's praise and greetings.

Putnam caught the next liner to join his wife and share, a bit eagerly perhaps, in the spotlight. Amelia was put through the lionizing process with which she was now wearily familiar— award ceremonies, luncheons, dinners, receptions. She stayed at the American Embassy with Andrew W. Mellon, the wizened financier who had been Secretary of the Treasury, and his fam-

ily. With all the awards and certificates and decorations raining
down on her, and all the evidence that she had joined the guild
of American heroes (Babe Ruth, Gertrude Ederle, Jack Demp-
sey, Lindbergh, Byrd, and a few less durable types), she seemed
a trifle disillusioned when she remarked, "If science advances
and aviation progresses, and international goodwill is promoted
because of my flight, no one will be more delighted than I—or
more surprised."

And it went on and on, from London to Paris to Rome, with
Putnam enjoying himself hugely and taking over at press conferences until one or two reporters wondered which of them
had flown the Atlantic, and Amelia's smile becoming more
fixed. In Paris she received the Cross of the Legion of Honor,
was given a reception by the French Senate, was entertained by
Elsa Maxwell and Lady Mendl (Elsie de Wolfe). In Rome they
were given an audience by Mussolini, who was gracious after
his own fashion to Amelia but a little frosty toward Putnam,
who several years before had published a book by a man who
had escaped from the Fascist prison island of Lipari. In Brussels
they were entertained privately by King Albert and the Belgian
royal family, and Amelia had the cross of a Chevalier of the
Order of Leopold pinned on the front of her dress.

The White House, on their return to America, could not be
outdone by European royalty. Amelia and her husband were
guests of President and Mrs. Herbert Hoover—a cheerless stay
because the President was preoccupied by the worsening depression and, unlike crowned heads, had to worry about the
forthcoming election. The Hoover household, Putnam remarked, was "pathetically dedicated to gloom." Nevertheless
Hoover spoke with more than usual warmth when he presented
Amelia with the gold medal of the National Geographic Society
at a full-dress affair in Constitution Hall the evening of June
21, 1932, one month after Amelia had made her first-woman's-
solo across the Atlantic.

Her flights and the manner in which she had conducted herself, the President said, "combine to place her in spirit with the

great pioneering women to whom every generation of Americans has looked up, with admiration for their firmness of will, their strength of character, and their cheerful spirit of comradeship in the work of the world." Amelia may have thought at that moment of her own pioneer grandparents, one set rich and comfortable on Quality Hill, the other scratching out a living on the sod-house frontier a few miles away.

"Her success," President Hoover went on, "has not been won by the selfish pursuit of a purely personal ambition, but as part of a career generously animated by a wish to help others to share in the rich opportunities of life, and by a wish also to enlarge those opportunities by expanding the powers of women as well as men to their ever-widening limits."

To the President, her achievements had demonstrated "new possibilities of the human spirit and the human will in overcoming barriers of space and the restrictions of Nature upon the radius of human activity."

Amelia made her low-keyed and modest reply that "the appreciation for the deed is out of proportion to the deed itself." No doubt she believed it. If she was a pioneer of the air age, there were other frontiers to be crossed.

12
An Addition of Laurels

THERE is something addictive about glory. If Amelia Earhart had an outsized ego, she concealed it well; yet she was always preoccupied with breaking new records, racking up new achievements. Something would not let her rest; something pushed her on to risk her life, time after time, in search of new conquests. It could not, like a virus, be isolated and studied under a microscope; the physiology of fame is something that needs a lot more investigation. Amelia herself could not describe the nature of the compulsion and knew only that it held her in an unbreakable grip.

Once, wistfully, she remarked to her sister, Muriel, how lucky the latter was in having children. For herself, it "took too long to make a baby." There were so many "exciting" things to be done in an airplane. Perhaps excitement was the virus that fevered her and would not allow her—unlike her male counterpart, Lindbergh, who was able to resist it and successfully seek a quieter, more meaningful life—to be content with what she had done, settle down, and be a housewife.

Instead she seemed to be intent on keeping her laurels fresh, obsessed with the magic of the statistics of record flights. Only three months after flying the Atlantic she established the women's nonstop transcontinental speed record, Los Angeles to New York in nineteen hours and five minutes. Eleven months later she broke her own record over the same course, flying it in seventeen hours and seven minutes.

Occasionally she would step out of the spotlight. Putnam's two sons would come to Rye on a visit and Amelia, determined to prove she wasn't the ogre type of stepmother, took them riding, picnicking, swimming, sailing on Long Island Sound. While the Putnam boys were visiting, she canceled all other social and professional engagements, and her big-sisterly, if not maternal, affection was returned.

Mostly, though, perhaps more to Putnam's taste than to that of his still self-effacing wife, they associated with celebrities of equal rank. Even the socially skittish Lindberghs were drawn into the Putnam orbit. They had been friends ever since Amelia wrote Mrs. Lindbergh apologizing for "the ridiculous 'Lady Lindy' publicity." Amelia added that "I believe I have never apologized so widely and so consistently for anything in my life, except possibly for having been born. The title was given me, I believe, probably because one or the other of us wasn't a swarthy runt. You understand my dislike of the title isn't because I don't appreciate being compared to one who has abilities such as Colonel Lindbergh has, but because that comparison is quite unjustified." When the Belgian Professor Auguste Piccard came to the United States after his high-altitude balloon experiments, Putnam invited him and the Lindberghs to a dinner at Putnam's house in Rye. There were several other guests. Putnam, knowing Lindbergh's horror of having anything he said or did reach the newspapers, was appalled a couple of days later when a New York paper provided a full account of the conversations around the Putnam dinner table. It turned out, on investigation, that Piccard's manager had sold the story for $40 in cash.

Amelia and her husband were also taken up socially by the new First Family, and Putnam, for one, found the White

House atmosphere during the early years of Franklin D. Roosevelt's residence more to his liking than during the Hoover administration. The clubbiness of the Roosevelt tenure, Putnam declared a trifle excessively, made F. D. R. and his family "very close indeed to the people of a thousand thousand other American families." To the Putnam family, at any rate. He and F. D. R. oozed charm over each other; Amelia and Eleanor Roosevelt were sympathetic because both had been social workers, both shared something of the same do-good spirit, and both regarded themselves as ugly duckling types.

Amelia, in fact, almost made Eleanor Roosevelt the First Flying First Lady.

The first intimation that the President's wife might, under Amelia's encouragement, be taking wing came in a story published by the Washington *Post*: "A slim, quiet woman in a white evening dress took Mrs. Roosevelt on a flight over Washington and Baltimore last night, piloting the big transport plane without even removing her long white kid gloves."

Amelia and her husband had dined at the White House that night, and later Amelia expanded to Mrs. Roosevelt on the peculiar fascination of flying at night, the sense of freedom, the communion with the starlit heavens. Noting that the venturesome First Lady was intensely interested in her description of night flying, Amelia impulsively asked her, "Would you like to try it?"

"Tonight?" Mrs. Roosevelt said.

"Why not?"

Without telling her own husband or Mrs. Roosevelt's, Amelia arranged to borrow a plane from Eastern Airlines. They sped out to the National Airport and took off with Amelia at the controls, Mrs. Roosevelt in the copilot's seat, several newspaperwomen and Mrs. Roosevelt's brother Hall back in the cabin.

Mrs. Roosevelt decided that she'd like to learn to fly herself —as privately as possible—with Amelia as her instructor. As required by law, she took a complete medical examination from a friend of Amelia's, Dr. Harry Templeton Smith. Mrs. Roosevelt then wrote Amelia: "I am enclosing my student pilot permit. Dr. Smith seemed to feel that I was all right. The question now comes as to whether I can induce my husband to let me take lessons. I will let you know if I am successful with him. I haven't had a chance even to talk to him about it."

Mrs. Roosevelt was a strong-minded woman who had her own way about a lot of things, but the President firmly quashed that project.

Being a quotable public figure did not inhibit Amelia from speaking her mind on controversial subjects, even when it went against the grain of accepted opinion. In the years when Nazism and Fascism were on the rise in Europe and Japan was taking the first jackbooted steps toward Pearl Harbor, via Manchuria, she expressed herself against all wars of any kind. Even in the mid-thirties most people did not believe there could be another world war, yet the possibility was becoming more real with every passing year. Amelia and Mrs. Caroline O'Day, a New York congresswoman who was a neighbor in Rye, were discussing the menacing news from abroad one day. Mrs. O'Day declared she was a pacifist and would probably be sentenced to a federal penitentiary if war came. "Me, too," said Amelia promptly. "I'll meet you at Atlanta."

Amelia was convinced that the fact that war had always been a "man's game," a chance for men to slip their leashes and escape from humdrum domesticity, was responsible for its surviving popularity. "The Crusades," she said, "would have been much less fun than the Crusaders found them if women had tagged along. And drafting women for the real work of war— not for the pretty, sideline jobs where you can wear giddy uniforms and not get dirtied up—would make war much less inviting to the males. Of course, once we got a serious discussion of such a draft, we should hear Chivalry crying out that females are much too frail to be subjected to the inhuman cruelties and hardships of what is, after all, 'a man's game.' Nonsense! Such a concept of Chivalry is hypocritical. Already it has blandly averted the men's gaze from the women who do so much of the world's dirty work—as often as not in the face of discrimination against their sex. . . . The trenches, combat service in the air, transport jobs in advanced positions, and even the other, less brilliant arenas of activity in the theater of war, are the last remaining strongholds of men. I suspect that men might rather vacate the arena altogether than share it with women."

She conveyed those convictions about war to a Daughters of the American Revolution convention in Washington. The DAR, given to stomping and waving their assegais on the subject of patriotism unqualified, had invited her to attend and speak. She not only was the descendant of a Revolutionary soldier on her father's side but had just received the Distinguished Flying Cross from Congress. That seemed to certify her reliability, even after she warned the Daughters they might not like what she said. Bluntly she told the DAR it was responsible to a large degree for getting the country into wars, and she ended up by saying they all ought to be drafted if there was another one. A deafening silence greeted her closing remarks.

There was a backlash against feminism in the United States during the thirties—the flappers with their rouged knees, the feminists with their bobbed hair had had their day during the previous decade, it was felt—but Amelia continued to expound her belief that women ought to be liberated from the kitchen and nursery on occasion and have their places taken by their menfolk. It was her contention—which the marriage counselors and sociologists adopted only after World War II and the explosive growth of the suburbs—that children in America saw far too little of their fathers. "I do think," she said, "American men are outstanding in their keen responsibility as providers. Now if they would only adopt the idea of getting into the kitchen once in a while, too, it seems to me they would be reasonably perfect." Fathers should become more intimately concerned with raising their children, with the result that they would be "better disciplined" and "more sensibly cared for."

If a woman had the skill and education to earn more than her husband, she demanded, "why should he not take over the home job, and with no sense of hurt pride? . . . I am convinced that in the long run it is good business for men to know more about home jobs than they generally do." Boys as well as girls, she added, should be taught domestic science in school.

She also went against prevailing opinion in regard to Prohibition at a time when most of the nation was celebrating repeal. She was proud to say, she told a Women's Christian Temperance Union convention, that she never used alcohol. "Until a better race is bred," she explained, "I fear prohibitory laws, such as those against murder, theft, etc., will have to be in force . . . people must be shown the evils of the liquor traffic. . . ."

But flying, not proselytizing, was her business, and she went out to win, to keep her unofficial championship, in any competition that offered itself. In the spring of 1933 women flyers were invited for the first time to join in the Bendix transcontinental race, with a top prize of $10,000. Both Amelia Earhart and Ruth Nichols promptly announced that they wanted to compete. The winning woman pilot, the race officials decided, would receive a special award of $2,000, with a consolation prize of $1,000 to the other woman contestant. "This inducement," as Ruth Nichols explained, "was offered to offset the fact that, although men pilots had been working for months to prepare for the race, Amelia and I were given only two weeks' notice." Miss Nichols considered that she was further handicapped because Amelia had her own Lockheed Vega available, while she had to spend half her preparatory time wangling the loan of a plane, a low-wing Lockheed Orion. It wasn't until the day before the race, in fact, that Miss Nichols got a chance to try out her plane.

Amelia's flight was dogged by bad breaks; she lost a hatch cover and had to come down for engine repairs, but she finished ahead of Miss Nichols, whose luck was even worse, and won the $2,000 women's prize.

A year later she was planning a flight from Hawaii to California, a venture which had been attempted by other pilots but never successfully. She would have to cross 2,400 miles of the Pacific. The lure, in part, was the $10,000 prize put up by a group of Hawaiian businessmen.

She sold her old Lockheed Vega, in which she had flown the Atlantic, to the Franklin Institute of Philadelphia for $8,000 and bought a new plane of the same make, similarly painted red to attract any air-sea rescue mission if she had to make a forced landing.

For the months preceding the flight she and her husband moved out to their Hollywood base. She had engaged as her technical adviser, navigational instructor, and engineering consultant the thirty-one-year-old Paul Mantz, who operated a small fleet of planes which he stunted for *Hell's Angels, Men with Wings,* and other films. Mantz was a Hollywood swashbuckler, a handsome, hard-living fellow who looked as much like an actor as any of those he impersonated. The son of a northern California school principal, Mantz had bluffed his way into the Army Air Corps on faked college credentials and was graduated as an aviation cadet at March Field. In addition to stunting for motion pictures, he also operated the "Honeymoon Express," which flew film stars on their elopements to Yuma or Las Vegas.

Aside from their German ancestry and their profession, two people could hardly have had less in common than Amelia Earhart and Paul Mantz. He was a professional daredevil, but he was also a highly skilled and scientific pilot, and Amelia respected that. They hit it off so well, in fact, that Mantz's jealous first wife brought up Amelia's name in a divorce trial a year and a half later. Under cross-examination Mantz testified that he merely acted as technical adviser on her flights. He admitted that Amelia twice had been a house guest at the Mantzes' home on Toluca Lake, California, once for a few days and another time for about a month, but "I never had a meal alone with her in my house and never stayed alone with her in the house at any time." Actually, Mantz was in love with and soon would marry the beautiful young widow of Roy Minor, another flier, who had a profile like Mary Astor's.

Just before Christmas, 1934, accompanied by Mantz and her husband, Amelia sailed for Honolulu aboard the Matson liner SS *Lurline*. Her plane was covered with a tarpaulin and lashed to the liner's forward deck. Reporters who greeted her when the ship docked wanted to know whether she was going to attempt the Hawaii-California flight, but Amelia refused to disclose her plans. Her passion for secrecy, her almost superstitious belief that talking about a project in advance tended to queer it, particularly if it was broadcast in the newspapers, was still unyielding.

Her closely watched preparations for the flight, however, made it apparent that she would attempt the California flight. She had to wait for the right weather conditions and for the go-ahead from Paul Mantz, who was testing the new Lockheed and all its engineering and navigational equipment.

The proposed flight soon became a center of controversy extending all the way back to Washington and New York. Her plane would take off from the Navy's Wheeler Field; that meant she would need Navy clearance. The Navy's experts on the scene, however, were balking because, they claimed, her plane's radio didn't have sufficient range to guarantee the safety of the flight. Mantz thereupon took the Lockheed up 12,000 feet and managed to contact a station at Kingman, Arizona— 3,000 miles to the east—on the plane's radio.

Then political complications arose. It was charged by business rivals of the group which had posted the $10,000 prize for the Hawaii-California flight that its actual purpose was to promote concessions on the U.S. tariff on sugar. *The Nation* and other mainland periodicals picked up the charge and voiced the suspicion that Amelia's reputation was being "bought" by the Hawaiian sugar interests. Further, it was asserted that after making her flight, if it was a success, she would be expected to use her prestige with Congress in obtaining a reduction of the sugar tariff.

The sponsors of the flight took alarm at all the editorial furor, which might indeed have an adverse effect on legislation pending in Congress. They called an emergency meeting, several days before Amelia was scheduled to take off, at the Royal Hawaiian Hotel in Honolulu. Amelia was summoned to appear in the private dining room.

Dressed in her leather jacket and jodhpurs, she drove in from Wheeler Field and listened to the sponsors propose that the flight be called off. Then she rose and told them: "I have no idea where the rumors of my political influence started. . . . My business is flying. I have spent nearly half of the sum you promised me to get my plane in condition and to bring it here, but I can soon recoup that loss.

"Gentlemen," she continued in a level, near-contemptuous tone, "there is an aroma of cowardice in this air. You know as well as I do that the rumor is trash, but if you can be intimidated, it might as well be true. Whether you live in fear or defend your integrity is your decision. I have made mine. I intend to fly to California within this next week, with or without your support."

She then stalked out of the room. Her sponsors plucked up their courage and decided not to back out of their promise of the prize money.

On January 11, 1935, she was all set for the takeoff, provided there was a break in the weather. It was squally around the islands that morning. At noon Amelia took a nap while her husband and Mantz consulted with the Navy's weather experts. At 3:30 the letter advised the flight's managers that there would be good weather along the projected course to California, but she'd have to take off before a line storm moved in from the west. If she delayed, Lieutenant E. W. Stevens of the meteorological office warned, she might be held up another ten days by a procession of tropical storms moving in from the central Pacific.

"Let's go, then," was Amelia's decision after listening to the weather forecast.

She drove out to Wheeler Field from the house at Waikiki where she had been a guest. The field was muddy from recent downpours. The Lockheed was heavily loaded but had a 6,000-foot runway for the takeoff. The 500 gallons of extra gasoline, the radio equipment, and other navigational aids brought the plane's weight up to three tons and over and would make it awkward to lift off the muddy runway.

At 4:30 P.M. she began to roll down the runway, laboriously gathered speed, struggled to get off the ground, and slowly began to lift. The worst part, Amelia thought, was over. She climbed to 5,000 feet and passed over Diamond Head, then gained another 2,000 feet of altitude. At least she wouldn't have to worry about fog or ice clogging her wings on this flight.

And the radio was functioning perfectly. As she flew through clear, starlit skies, she maintained radio contact with Hawaiian stations at half-hour intervals. With the map on her knees, she checked the position of various ships along her course, which were supposed to turn on their searchlights if they heard her passing overhead. By midnight she was 900 miles out from Wheeler Field.

The Matson liner *Maliko* spotted her, turned on her searchlight, was answered by blinking from the Lockheed's landing lights, and radioed the plane's position to Honolulu. In the early-morning hours she was entertained by snatches of a broadcast of the San Francisco Symphony Orchestra. The engine was functioning perfectly; the weather was holding clear, and she celebrated with a postmidnight supper of malted milk tablets and hot chocolate from a thermos bottle.

Just after sunrise Amelia spotted a large passenger ship 8,000 feet below. Circling it several times, she learned it was the Dollar liner *President Pierce,* San Francisco-bound from Honolulu. She lined up her plane with the ship's mile-long wake and learned that her navigation through the night via compass had been absolutely accurate.

By radio she contacted radio station KPO in San Francisco and learned that the *President Pierce* was just 300 miles off the California coast.

Shortly before noon she sighted the coastal mountains of California, turned north, and caught a glimpse of the waters of San Francisco Bay. A few minutes later she was touching down at the Bay Farm Island Airport near Oakland. The flight from Honolulu had taken eighteen hours and fifteen minutes—and it was a real first for any flier, male or female. Ten thousand people, having been alerted by newspaper and radio reports of her progress, were waiting to cheer and mob her. It was the longest flight she had ever made, and she was somewhat surprised to find herself wobbling from weariness when she jumped out of the plane. She managed to give the crowd the expected Earhart grin, then a large police escort opened a path to the waiting car and a round-the-clock sleep.

13
Untarnished Golden Girl

*A*MELIA'S modesty was undiminished by the praise raining down on her for the Pacific flight. Nothing embarrassed her more than excessive praise or irritated her more than an undeserved compliment. She kept a file labeled BUNK for hymns to her valor and messages of fulsome flattery which she regarded as making her seem ridiculous by going too far. One prize specimen was the telegram from the mayor of a large city, which ululated over the prospect of a visit from her: "Welcome, thrice welcome, grand lady of the air, crowned glory of earth's womanhood."

Sir Anthony Jenkinson was one of the guests, along with Amelia, at a dinner at the home of Paul Hammond less than a month after the Pacific flight. On February 5, 1935, he noted in his journal (quoted in his memoir *America Comes My Way*) that he was seated next to Miss Earhart at the Santa Monica dinner party and found her "so modest, so natural, and so feminine." Somehow, he recorded, "one expects ocean fliers to be grim, tight-lipped people, but Miss Earhart is gay, smiling and friendly. Clearly hers is a mental rather than a physical courage, giving effect, not to bulging muscles and a philosophy of reckless, senseless daring, but rather to abundant confidence, poise, and a firm, purposeful character.

"This evening was, I think, the first time Miss Earhart had been informally amongst friends since she landed at Los Angeles last week after her Pacific flight. She brought along with her the chart she used for the flight. It was about 2½ feet long and 8 inches wide and divided up into little sections, each of which represented one hour's flying. In each section—before the flight started—information and instructions relative to that particular hour's flying had been written. These instructions included the necessary alterations of the course to be made at the end of each hour.

" 'You see,' she said with a modest laugh, 'the chart made navigation dead easy. All I had to do was to follow the written instructions at the end of every hour.' "

Along with that inherent modesty went the compulsion to accept any challenge that presented itself in the field of aviation. Only three months after the Pacific flight she was winging her way solo from Los Angeles to Mexico City, another first. Lindbergh of course had flown from Washington to Mexico City in 1927. The idea for the flight came from the President of Mexico—the first time a government had invited her. The challenge came from the veteran flier Wiley Post, who had become a friend of hers, although he didn't mean it as a dare.

Discussing the proposed Mexican flight with Post, she explained that she intended to fly to the Mexican capital from Los Angeles, then from Mexico City to Newark. On the return flight she would use the most direct route, across the Gulf of Mexico.

"That's about seven hundred miles," he protested. "Almost half an Atlantic. How much time do you lose if you go around by the shore?"

"About an hour," she replied.

"Amelia, don't do it," he said earnestly. "It's too dangerous."

Amelia said later she could hardly believe her ears. "Did Wiley Post, the man who had braved every sort of hazard in his stratosphere flying, really regard a simple little flight from Mexico City to New York across the Gulf as too hazardous? If so, I could scarcely wait to be on my way." What may really have made her determined to make the flight was the reflection that Post considered the flight too dangerous *for a woman;* that would make it a challenge indeed. If her aerial exploits were to some extent compulsive, it was because she felt it necessary to prove a woman could earn and hold her place in a man's world, and there was no more masculine sphere of influence than flying.

There was no doubt that she was urged on by a strong compulsion to prove women could compete on equal terms with men. The first time Louise Thaden met her, Amelia made that clear. Mrs. Thaden, a handsome, firm-jawed woman who combined motherhood with a flying career, was a tyro with only a hundred hours in the air at the time. They met at the Oakland airport shortly after Amelia's first Atlantic flight; her charismatic quality was evidenced by the fact that "every male pilot at the airport," as Mrs. Thaden recalled, was sitting or standing around her in a close huddle.

Mrs. Thaden finally managed a few minutes alone with her idol. "We women pilots," Amelia told her, "have a rough, rocky road ahead of us. Each accomplishment, no matter how small, is important. Although it may be no direct contribution to the science of aeronautics or its technical development, it will encourage other women to fly. The more women who fly, the more who become pilots, the quicker we will be recognized as an important factor in aviation."

When Mrs. Thaden got to know her better, she was convinced that Amelia's feminism was stronger than any yearnings for personal recognition or advancement. Amelia had "an insatiable desire to get women into the air. . . . I have known many women pilots she has helped either through financial assistance or moral encouragement." Using the influence she and Putnam had acquired at the White House, Amelia conducted a two-year campaign to persuade the Bureau of Air Commerce to employ women as pilots, which finally succeeded when the bureau took on Louise Thaden. Tokenism, but better than nothing.

Once Amelia and Mrs. Thaden dined together, and the latter asked, "Just what *do* you want?"

"Recognition for women," Amelia replied immediately. "Men do not believe us capable. We can fly—you know that. Ever since we started we've batted our heads against a stone wall. Manufacturers refuse us planes. The public have no confidence in our ability. If we had access to the equipment and training men have, we could certainly do as well. Thank heaven, we continue willingly fighting a losing battle. Every year we pour thousands of dollars into flight training with no hope of return. A man can work, or he can join the Army. When he has a license he can obtain a flying job to build up his time. A man can borrow the latest equipment for special flights or records; and what do we get? Obsolete airplanes. And why? Because we are women seldom are we trusted to do an efficient job."

There is no reason to believe that Amelia Earhart, if she were alive today, would be dismayed by any of the more extravagant methods of the third wave of the feminist movement, which began cresting late in the sixties.

The Mexico City flight was one more attempt at proving that women had earned the right to take the controls of the latest aircraft and use the most advanced equipment.

Once again she favored night flying, perhaps more because of its poetic than its practical aspects. In talking about the Mexican venture later with Paul Gallico—then sports editor of the New York *Daily News,* later a best-selling author, and a man she particularly liked—she indicated that she was strongly influenced by the visual delights of being in the air, the poetry of flight. "She pulled an enchanting feminine line when we were discussing what pilots think about on those long, lonely transcontinental and ocean hops when there is nothing to do but hold the ship level and let her fly herself. 'Do you know,' she said, 'the only thing I can remember thinking about the flight up from Mexico City was while crossing the Gulf of Mexico. Clusters of thunderstorms were beginning to stick their heads up. I cut around the edges of the thunderheads, and they had purple lightning inside. And all I could think was, 'How pretty my ship must look against such a background—and there is nobody here to see it.' "

She particularly loved flying at night, alone with the stars, and had done so on both the Atlantic and Hawaii-California flights. On the flight from Burbank, California, to Mexico City she took off shortly before midnight on April 19, 1935. The moonscape over the Southwest did not disappoint her. Later she wrote of a "generous moon which gilded the hills gloriously. . . . Even the mechanical difficulties which beset the early hours of the flight—chiefly an engine which overheated because of a faulty propeller setting—could not mar the rare loveliness of the night and of the farflung countryside which slumbered beneath."

Some of her exaltation at getting off the ground may have been traceable to the controversy which had attended her husband's method of financing the flight. Fame, it seemed, had a way of generating controversy; the pedestal often merely made one a handy target. On Lindbergh's flight to Mexico City he had been accused of making propaganda for the American oil interests, not by anything he said but because his flight increased goodwill at a time when the oilmen were threatened with sequestration of their properties. In Amelia's case, her flight was partly financed by the issuance of special Mexican stamps and by autographed letter covers, which she carried in her Lockheed. Seven hundred and eighty stamps were overprinted with "Amelia Earhart, *Vuelo de buena voluntad Mexico 1935.*"

An involved dispute arose among stamp dealers, often a contentious lot, over the Amelia Earhart issue; and George Putnam had to make a statement defending the integrity of the operation: "When the Mexican Government graciously suggested the issue, and offered me the privilege of purchasing some of it, it readily agreed that every precaution was to be taken against possible fraud. The stamp was overprinted from electro cuts deliberately designed to forestall copying. The overprinting was done in violet ink which, against the red background of the stamp itself, precluded photography and made copying exceedingly difficult. I personally was present and saw all the 780 stamps printed. The cuts used were never out of my sight. After the printing these cuts were destroyed in my presence, all as attested by affidavits of witnessing officials. In short, I tried to do everything possible to insure the absolute integrity of the issue."

During the early stage of the flight, while negotiating the Gulf of California, Amelia was troubled by a white haze which made it difficult to differentiate between the water and the horizon. Her engine overheated, but she managed to correct that by resetting the propeller.

Otherwise the flight proceeded smoothly, and she was bang on target reaching Mazatlán, her checkpoint, about a thousand miles from the Burbank airport. At Mazatlán, according to her chart, she was to turn east and fly over the high plateaus and the mountains of central Mexico to the capital. From an altitude of 10,000 feet she spotted the towns of Guadalajara and Tepic. The morning hours droned by. Her estimated time of arrival at Mexico City was about 1 P.M. Mexican time.

When that hour passed and there was no sign of Mexico City, she became somewhat concerned. She had to find out where she was, so she picked out what looked like a level place and descended. It turned out to be a dry lakebed, dotted with cactus and prickly pear. Within minutes after her plane rolled to a stop, men on horseback came out from the nearby village. There was a language barrier; she couldn't speak Spanish, and the horsemen couldn't speak English. She showed her map to a bright-looking youth, and they made out through sign language. Pointing to the map, he indicated she had landed outside the village of Nopala. Mexico City was about fifty miles away.

Half an hour later she landed at the airport outside the capital and was given an enthusiastic welcome. Even President Cárdenas, officially unfriendly toward gringos and busy expropriating American oil companies, extended his greetings. She was taken to the floating gardens of Xochimilco, to jai alai games and fiestas, but was disappointed, as a flying feminist, in not being able to meet more of the Mexican women and discuss their problems. She saw only the "sheltered women among the well-to-do," as an official guest of the government, and "only briefly touched a few groups of self-supporting city women workers." It did not bother her that many Americans were embittered by Cárdenas' policies toward American property because of her hope for "reforms the new order holds for its women."

As it turned out, she had to spend eight days in Mexico City before receiving the telegraphed go-ahead from her friend, Dr. Kimball, in the New York Weather Bureau. Meanwhile, the Mexican army was clearing a three-mile runway for her heavily loaded plane on the mud flats of what had once been the bottom of Lake Texcoco outside Mexico City.

She received the favorable weather bulletin shortly after midnight on May 8 and decided to make the return flight immediately. Driving at once out to Lake Texcoco, she watched while drums of gasoline were poured into her Lockheed's tanks; for her own sustenance her Mexican friends had provided enough food for a dozen flights: hard-boiled eggs, sandwiches, tomato juice, and a thermos of coffee. A Pan American Airways mechanic gave her engine its final checkup under the headlights of an automobile parked as close to the cowling as possible.

For all of Wiley Post's forebodings, this was the least troubled of all her long-distance flights. Her engine drumming steadily, she flew over Tampico, then headed northeast over the Gulf of Mexico to New Orleans. She was in constant radio communication with the ground stations.

Crossing the 700-mile stretch of water, she later recorded, she first thought of the possibility of using a larger, two-engined plane. There was nothing but blue water from horizon to horizon, and "one's imagination toyed with the thought of what would happen if the single engine of the Lockheed Vega should conk. Not that my faithful Wasp ever had failed me, or indeed, even protested mildly. . . . On that sunny morning out of the sight of land, I promised my lovely red Vega I'd fly her across no more water. And I promised myself that any further over-ocean flying would be attempted in a plane with more than one motor, capable of keeping aloft with a single engine. Just in case. . . ."

This flight, however, went off with a "delightful precision." From New Orleans she followed her flight plan up the line to Mobile, Atlanta, Charlotte, Richmond, Washington. When she passed over Washington, her old friend Gene Vidal was standing by at the ground station and told her by radio, "You've done enough. You'd better land at Hoover Airport."

"No, thanks," Amelia replied. "I'm going through to New York."

Thousands, including her husband and Dr. Kimball, were waiting to greet her when she landed, fourteen hours and nineteen minutes after taking off from Mexico City, at Newark Airport. The crowd overflowed the field and mobbed her plane before she could wearily clamber out of the cockpit. The painful aspect of mass adulation soon presented itself. A flying wedge of policemen forced its way to her rescue. One cop had her by the right arm, another had taken a firm grip on her left leg, and Amelia became the victim of a tug-of-war.

For a few minutes, she said, she knew "the fleeting taste of the tortures of the rack" until her rescuers sorted themselves out and hauled her through the screaming mob and into a police car. Now she could appreciate some of Lindbergh's feelings about idolatrous crowds, who sometimes seemed to be looking for a blood sacrifice, but she took care not to show it.

The association with flamboyant Paul Mantz continued later that year. She and the Hollywood stunt flier had talked about starting a flying school. At his insistence they drew up a formal agreement. "We're in a dangerous business, Amelia," he told her. "We'd better put it all on paper in case one of us is killed." The Earhart-Mantz Flying School never got off the drawing board, however.

Another joint effort was entering the 1935 National Air Races promoted by Cliff Henderson. The first five to finish in the race to Cleveland over the Labor Day weekend would receive cash prizes, and Mantz was confident their entry would place in the money.

Each had a Lockheed Vega, so they flipped a coin to see which plane would make the race. Amelia won the toss. Again she was impressed by Mantz's analytical intelligence when it came to judging the performance of planes and pilots. Admittedly, their Vega didn't stand much of a chance of winning. At least two of their rivals would be flying hotter aircraft, Roscoe Turner in his sleek Weddell-Williams and Benny Howard's *Mister Mulligan*, a high-wing cabin plane; and both Turner and Howard were crack racing pilots. Other entries included Jacqueline Cochran, appearing in her first Bendix race, and Russell Thaw, the personal pilot for the Guggenheim family, both flying Northrop Gammas. Roy O. Hunt had entered with a Lockheed Orion; Earl Ortman with an R-3 Keith Rider Silver Bullet, an all-metal plane with a 750-horsepower Wasp engine; Cecil Allen and Royal Leonard with Gee Bee racing planes. Allen's plane was sponsored by a mysterious backer known only as Mrs. C. L. D.

Amelia was to pilot her Lockheed in the race to Cleveland, with Mantz and his friend Al Menasco, an engine builder, going along for the ride. Just before takeoff, shortly after midnight, Mantz handed Amelia a slip of paper on which he had handicapped all the entries. On the flight Mantz and Menasco sat back in the cabin playing gin rummy while Amelia, eager for all the long-distance time she could get, did the flying.

The Earhart-Mantz entry finished fifth and won the $500 prize, which paid their expenses. Shortly after they had taxied to the hangar at the Cleveland airport, Amelia opened the slip

Mantz had given her and found that Mantz had called the shots. He'd predicted Turner and Howard would finish one-two (Howard had won by twenty-three seconds), that Thaw and Hunt would take third and fourth places, which they did, and that he and Amelia would come in fifth. And on his scratch sheet, opposite Cecil Allen's name, Mantz had drawn a small wreath. Sure enough, they learned a few minutes later that Allen had crashed on takeoff. It was things like that which made her respect Mantz's judgment, his knowledge of men and machines.

During the later part of 1935 Amelia decided to seek a more secluded and less active life for a time. She needed time and peace of mind to decide what her next move would be. Even while flying up from Mexico earlier in the year, part of her mind had been focused on the possibility of circumnavigating the earth in a multiengined plane. The chanciness of further and riskier ventures, balanced against her ambitions, also had to be taken into consideration. That year Wiley Post and Will Rogers were killed when their plane crashed in Alaska.

The modern version of the cloister is the university, and it was that form of retreat she finally chose. The previous year she had addressed a conference sponsored by the New York *Herald Tribune* on the subject of "Women and the Changing World." She was presented to the conference by Mrs. William Brown Meloney, a magazine editor, as evidence that "no generation which could produce Amelia Earhart can be called a lost generation." In her own speech Amelia jolted some of her listeners by declaring it was time attention was paid "young ideas" rather than "elders" such as herself whom the world "decidedly has on the run" because of continuing threats of war and the economic depression. Later she and her husband dined with Dr. Edward C. Elliott, the president of Purdue University, at the Coffee House, a mid-Manhattan club with a rather special membership (then as now) with liberal/progressive/radical political and social tendencies. During a long conversation at the table and later in the lounge, Dr. Elliott brought up the idea of having Amelia attach herself to the Indiana university's faculty. She pointed out that she had no degrees or other qualifications for teaching in a classroom. Dr. Elliott replied that eight hundred of Purdue's students were girls, and Amelia could inspire them in informal seminars, "supply some spark" which would leap between the real world and the classroom.

Amelia pondered that invitation during the next year and after her Mexican flight decided to accept. On June 2, 1935, President Elliott announced to the university that she would join the faculty the following autumn as exemplar of "what may be called the new pioneering."

As aviatrix in residence, she moved into one of the women's dormitories, spoke informally to groups of students, dined at a different table every night, and kept her door open to girls who wanted to discuss their problems, their hopes of shaping a career, not necessarily in aviation. From all accounts she was a huge success, and given her attitude, her straight-from-the-shoulder style, would probably have been as popular today as she was in 1935-36.

Certainly in that year her candor was striking.

"Many divorces," she told one group of coeds, "are caused by the complete dependence of the female. At first there is the strong sexual attraction that sometimes masquerades as love. Everything goes well until the first financial crisis jars the man's confidence and threatens the woman's security. The woman can't help. All she can be is dependent, because that is what she has been trained to be. Instead of standing beside the man, giving him encouragement by contributing her own efforts, she becomes accusatory and sullen and the sex drive that passed for love is no longer enough to satisfy either of them. . . . If we begin to think and respond as capable human beings able to deal with and even enjoy the challenges of life, then we surely will have something more to contribute to marriage than our bodies. We must earn true respect and equal rights from men by accepting responsibilities."

She startled some of the mossier pedants on the faculty by advocating that higher education move into closer touch with realities—relevance would be the later campus cliché for it. She foresaw, in fact, "the entire reconstruction of our educational system," explaining: "Because Johnny liked to play with tin soldiers, his mother has jumped to the conclusion, since the year one, that he wanted to be a soldier! So she packed him off to military school—which he hated—though maybe she never found it out—all because what really interested him about tin soldiers was that they were made of lead, and lead is metal, and you heat metal and melt it and make it into lots of things— steel for skyscrapers, decorative ironwork, leading for stained-glass windows."

As for the female students, she felt they needed, and would increasingly need, the "critical stimulus of competition outside the home." This was a slightly heretical belief at a time when women were being encouraged to stay at home and not compete for the few jobs available.

Her venturesome ideas pleased Dr. Elliott, however, and Purdue regarded itself as an experimental as well as an educational institution. The university had its own airport, for instance, at which students could learn to fly at reduced rates for instruction.

Still, it was rather surprising that the Purdue Research Foundation, acting under Amelia's stimulating personality and Dr. Elliott's enthusiastic backing, decided to set up the Amelia Earhart Fund. The chief function of that fund, as it turned out, was to purchase a new plane which she would use as a flying laboratory. Fifty thousand dollars was set aside for the purpose. On March 20, 1936, the most advanced of nonmilitary aircraft then in existence was ordered, a twin-engine, dual-control, ten-passenger Lockheed 10-E Electra, with a gasoline capacity of 1,204 gallons and a range of 4,500 miles. Obviously it wasn't designed for flying around the cow pastures and woodlots of southern Indiana.

The more or less academic purpose of the "flying laboratory" was to study "the effect of flying on people." Putnam said she was to "have a free hand working out continuous problems arising from her own experience in aviation." In accepting the plane, Amelia herself told the trustees and President Elliott that her ambition was to "produce practical results for the future of commercial flying and for the women who may want to fly tomorrow's planes."

She took delivery of the plane on her thirty-eighth birthday, July 24, 1936, and on the Department of Commerce's application for a license listed as its designated use: "Long distance flights and research." That was closer to the mark. From that day on she began preparing herself and her new plane for one last coup: a flight around the world.

14
In Training

WHILE preparing herself for one last great effort—the greatest challenge in aviation at the time—Amelia became friendly with Jacqueline Cochran, the glamour girl of that first generation of women fliers. Miss Cochran, who had scrambled her way up from a Florida sawmill town, headed her own cosmetics firm and was married to the financier Floyd Odlum. Next to Amelia Earhart and Ruth Nichols, she was probably the best known of the women pioneers of the air.

She and her husband lived on a palatial estate near Indio in the California desert. Since Amelia was making Los Angeles the headquarters of her preparations, she and Putnam were frequent guests of Miss Cochran and her husband. Once the latter accompanied Amelia on a test flight from New York to California in the new Lockheed Electra.

During that flight, which took six days because they were frequently forced down by bad weather, the two women discovered that each had acquired a near-obsessive interest in extrasensory perception. Psychic phenomena had long been an avocation with both Miss Cochran and her husband. Amelia, however, had become interested in ESP through recently having learned of Dr. J. B. Rhine's work at Duke University. This, of course, was long before Dr. Rhine's work became well known or ESP the subject of wide public fascination.

Shortly after the transcontinental tuneup flight Amelia went to the Odlum ranch near Indio for a few days' rest, and while there the opportunity arose for some personal investigation of extrasensory perception. "The first night there," wrote Miss Cochran in her autobiography, *The Stars at Noon,* "we heard that a passenger plane had disappeared en route from Los Angeles to Salt Lake City and Amelia asked me to try to locate it. We sat together for about two hours during which I gave names of various mountain peaks and the location of roads and transmission lines and even a pile of telephone poles up in the mountains near Salt Lake City. I also gave the location of the plane. Neither of us knew that area so Amelia called Paul Mantz in Los Angeles and asked him to verify names and locations on an air map and call us back. He called back with complete verification. Amelia, thoroughly excited by that time, dashed back to Los Angeles by car through the night and took off for Salt Lake City in her plane at daybreak. She searched the area for three days and verified all my descriptions but found no wreckage of the transport and gave up. Next spring, when the snow on the mountain had melted, the wreckage of that plane was found within two miles of where, on the night it went down, I said it was."

A few weeks later, Miss Cochran has related, another airliner went down en route to Los Angeles. Amelia called her and asked her to determine the location by ESP. Miss Cochran not only supplied the location, she said, but the number of dead, injured, and uninjured. All the information proved to be correct.

By then Amelia was a true believer. She was convinced that if she happened to be forced down on her proposed globe-girdling flight, Jacqueline Cochran would be able to direct rescuers where to find her. On one of her subsequent transcontinental flights Amelia agreed, as an experiment, to keep a record every hour on the hour of where she was. Miss Cochran, exercising her ESP, would do likewise. "But I became engaged in some cosmetic problem," Miss Cochran recalled, "and forgot until Floyd jacked up my memory on the third day. I then told Floyd what Amelia had been doing that day and he sent the report on to her.

"It was that she (and her husband George Putnam, who was with her) had landed the night before at Blackwell, Oklahoma; that it was fifty miles off their course because they had become confused by weather and radio; that they took off at nine o'clock in the morning for Los Angeles but stopped in Winslow, Arizona, for refueling.

"George Putnam wrote back that I had certainly made a bad miss that time. He said that while they did stop at Blackwell overnight, it was not because they were lost; that they took off at seven o'clock and not nine o'clock but that I did hit it right in saying that they stopped at Winslow for gas. George Putnam really confirmed the case. I didn't know what part of the country they were in at the time and had never heard the name Blackwell; seven o'clock their time was nine o'clock my New York time; and whether one is lost or not is more or less a state of mind as to which pilots differ. A favorite expression of the old-time barnstorming pilots used to be: 'I ain't lost but I don't know where I'm at.' "

Miss Cochran was offended by the tone of Putnam's letter and admittedly was "never too fond of him" anyway, but "I loved Amelia with a deep, true and loyal affection. She was a greater flyer and an even greater woman." Amelia spent much time at the Odlum ranch getting in shape for the round-the-world trip, swimming and horseback riding. Part of the financing for that venture, in fact, came from the Odlums, and Amelia dedicated her last book, *Last Flight*, "to Floyd with gratitude for all-weather friendship."

Behind that project, as Amelia avowed, there was a sober scientific purpose. She proposed to make a "human guinea pig" of herself and "test human reactions" to long-distance flights.

The aircraft industry, including both the commercial airlines and the plane manufacturers, had concentrated on mechanical problems and the economic feasibility of providing mass transportation in the air. "I am interested," she said, "in finding out whether one kind of food is better than another during flight; i.e., the effects of altitude on metabolism. Also I should like to know the rate at which fatigue is induced by the myriad instruments a modern pilot must use. What will stratosphere flying do to creatures accustomed to the dense air of lower altitudes? Are men and women different in their reactions to air travel? If so, how? And perhaps, why?"

She was particularly concerned with her belief that other considerations—principally safety—had been sacrificed in the preoccupation with speed. She even considered the possibility that aircraft designers and manufacturers might go back to the first flying machines and study their reliability, flimsy though they were. Not faster but slower flight should be attempted, at least in some models. She thought a plane should be developed that flew at forty miles an hour, with a landing speed of thirty. The profusion of instruments in the cockpits of the newer planes also bothered her. On her new Electra there were more than a hundred dials and levers and indicators "I either have to look at or twiddle."

Preparations, she believed, were responsible for two-thirds of the success of any long and dangerous flight. So she prepared with greater diligence than ever before for the round-the-world venture; to the flier it represented what Mount Everest did to the mountain climber. The late Wiley Post had flown around the world twice in his Lockheed Vega in 1931 and 1933. In 1935 he and Will Rogers set out for Post's third flight around the world, which ended when his nose-heavy Lockheed Orion crashed into the Alaskan tundra and killed both men. Lindbergh and his wife had conducted an aerial survey of South America, Europe, and Africa in 1933. The following year Charles Kingsford-Smith and Captain P. G. Taylor made the first flight from Australia to California.

Amelia's project, however, was more daring than any of those. While Post's flights had been made north of the equator, Amelia's would circle the earth roughly *at* the equator, a much longer distance of about 27,000 miles. The route she originally laid out was east to west, from Oakland to Honolulu to Howland Island in the central Pacific to Port Darwin in northern Australia, then from Australia to Africa via Arabia, across the South Atlantic to Brazil, and back to the United States.

Obviously she would need a navigator, one who knew celestial navigation, who could guide her across long trackless stretches of ocean. On her previous flights she had "dead-reckoned" her way to landfall, but "then I was aiming at continents, not small spots of land in the mightiest ocean."

And there were other preparations which had to be made long before she took off on the first leg of the flight. Mostly these were in charge of her husband, who arranged with Standard Oil to have gasoline cached around the whole route of her flights and with Pratt & Whitney for spare parts wherever they might be needed. Putnam also had to obtain clearances from the embassies of the various countries where she would land or which she would fly over to avoid any charges of aerial trespassing. A small corps of experts was working on various other problems. Paul Mantz again was the technical adviser (at a fee of $100 a day), and Clarence S. Williams of Los Angeles prepared all the maps and charts she would need.

Money was getting to be a problem, as Putnam wrote Mantz. "It may interest you to know," he added, "that it looks as if the airlines, jointly and entirely on their own, are going to do something for AE. They seem to recognize her as the most important single agency in America today popularizing air travel. Especially combatting feminine sales resistance. Which would be nice and fair enough, if it comes through. As usual, she is asking for nothing."

Mantz, however, had plenty to worry about in the mechanical line and was particularly concerned about the problem of pilot fatigue. With all his respect for Amelia's capabilities, he wasn't at all certain that a woman could stand up to the long hours of staying at the controls during a globe-girdling flight. "A Sperry Robot Pilot," he wrote Putnam, "is essential; it will eliminate fifty percent of her fatigue." He also insisted that her instrumental flying must be more precise and disciplined and installed a Link blind-flying trainer, which simulated the actual conditions of flight in a closed cockpit, in his Burbank hangar for endless hours of putting Amelia through her paces.

Mantz consulted Clarence M. Belinn, an old friend of Amelia's and engineering superintendent for National Airways in Boston, on how to increase the Electra's range for long ocean hops. Belinn was an expert on cross-feed problems and was willing to design a special system of auxiliary tanks to boost her fuel capacity.

Belinn, later president of Los Angeles Airways, the first of the helicopter short-haul lines, recalls that he then considered Amelia to be living on borrowed time because of something he learned following her 1932 solo across the Atlantic. Her old Lockheed Vega was returned to the Boston Airport for a checkup. Belinn found that all four of the brackets which attached the wing to the fuselage were cracked due to metal fatigue—and, he adds, "I mean cracked to the 'yield' point."

For her round-the-world flight Belinn obtained wing tanks from cannibalizing decommissioned planes, three on each wing, plus six more installed inside the fuselage, and worked out a cross-feed system between the auxiliaries and the main tank which Amelia could operate through a master valve on the floor of the cockpit.

She would now have a capacity of 1,200 gallons which "gave her a range of 2,500 to 3,000 miles depending on wind resistance," Belinn has recalled.

At the end of 1936 Mantz was fairly satisfied with the plane and confident of its performance but admittedly was worried about pilot fatigue and navigation. He wondered whether Amelia was in prime condition, considering the fact that she had delivered 136 lectures that year, among all her other activities. He worried about whether she was being pushed too far too fast. Navigating a plane around the world took a combination of skills which few men possessed.

For navigation, celestial and otherwise, Captain Harry Manning of the SS *Roosevelt,* who years before had been awarded the Congressional Medal of Honor for rescuing thirty-two passengers from the sinking liner *Florida,* and who had become a close personal friend, had volunteered to accompany the flight. On the first leg from Oakland to Australia they would have the services of Fred Noonan, who had been a Pan American Airways pilot and navigator and who would relieve Amelia at the controls over the longer stretches of ocean flying and also help Captain Manning with the navigation.

Early in 1937 everything seemed to be ready. Amelia had trained herself like an athlete; her mechanical experts had tuned the Electra to the top pitch of performance.

On February 11, at a press conference summoned by her husband in the Hotel Barclay in New York, she announced her plans for the global flight. She was dressed in a dark blue woolen dress with a scarf tied around her throat, and Captain Manning was at her side. "Well," she told the reporters, "I'm going to try to fly around the globe as near the equator as I can make it, east to west, about twenty-seven thousand miles." She traced her route on a globe while newsreel cameramen and newspaper photographers closed in to take their pictures.

"You know," she remarked with a slightly nervous laugh, "I feel you men have pushed me into this. You're the ones who have kept saying and saying that I was going to fly around the world until finally you've compelled me to think seriously about doing it."

She was kidding, of course, but one of the reporters snapped at the bait. "Oh, come on now," he said, "nobody has pushed you into it. You know you've been wanting to do it all the time."

Amelia grinned and replied, "Yes, I suppose you're right. I didn't get away with it, did I?"

"What are you really going for?" another reporter asked.

The question, oddly, seemed to stump her for a moment, and she glanced over at Captain Manning as though he might be able to explain. Then haltingly she made an attempt at explaining what was probably inexplicable, at least within the narrow confines of a press conference. "Well, I've seen the North Atlantic," she said. "I've seen the Pacific too, of course, at least part of it. But—well, just say I want to fly around the globe. And I think a round-the-world flight just now should be at the equator. Captain Manning is going with me partway because I don't believe the pilot on such a flight can navigate too." The last leg of the flight, Brazil to the United States, would be made solo.

A certain amount of controversy arose over the flight and over all such attempts to expand man's mastery over the planet. Some of her closest friends in aviation were dubious about the merits of her flight plan, about her plane's ability to negotiate such long distances over water. Touching down at Paterson Field on a cross-country jaunt, she was cornered by several of her female colleagues at lunch in the officers' club and bluntly told she ought to abandon her project. She admitted it was risky with the kind of radio equipment obtainable as a civilian and that government regulations forbade her borrowing Army or Navy radios.

But Amelia, after listening to their objections, only shook her head and said, "I have to meet my obligations."

Jacqueline Cochran has revealed how her own doubts about the feasibility of the venture grew as takeoff time neared. "I had plenty of 'hunches' about that flight," she wrote, referring to her extrasensory powers, "and none of them was on the optimistic side."

More to the point, perhaps, was a premonitory episode instigated by Miss Cochran herself. "I questioned whether the navigator she had employed, although an exceedingly fine man, was up to high-speed celestial navigation in a plane." Conning a liner at twenty-two knots, after all, was greatly different from navigating a plane at 200-plus miles an hour. "I asked her to take him out to sea for quite a distance from Los Angeles and then, after flying in circles for a time so he could no longer be oriented, to ask him to give her the course back to Los Angeles. She told me they reached the shore line halfway between Los Angeles and San Francisco." That would have been at least 200 miles off course.

Another female colleague with misgivings about the venture was Louise Thaden, who flew out to Burbank in January, 1937, to discuss the matter with Amelia. She found Amelia out at the Union Air Terminal near Paul Mantz's hangar, under siege from a group of autograph hunters. When Amelia disentangled herself from her admirers, she and Mrs. Thaden walked arm in arm to an office Amelia used in the hangar.

"Look here," Mrs. Thaden said sternly, "you've gone crazy on me. Why stick your neck out a mile on this round-the-world flight? You don't need to do anything anymore. You're tops now and if you never do anything else you always will be. It seems to me you've got everything to lose and nothing to gain."

They sat down on a rubber life raft, and Amelia replied, "You're a fine one to be talking to me like that. Aren't you the gal who flew in last year's Bendix with a gas tank draped around your neck?"

More seriously, she explained to Mrs. Thaden: "I've wanted to do this flight for a long time. . . . I've worked hard and I deserve one fling during my lifetime. . . . If I should bop off, it will be doing the thing I've always wanted most to do. Being a fatalist yourself you know. The Man with the little black book has a date marked down for all of us—when our work here is finished. . . ."

Aside from her friends' reactions and doubts and premonitions, a certain amount of public resistance was cropping up; so many lives had been lost in aerial adventures that seemed, on reflection, to prove nothing but the extent of human self-confidence. Even those who made a career of flying were having

their doubts about the heroic age of aviation. These were suc-
cinctly voiced in a *Saturday Evening Post* article a year and a
half later (October 22, 1938) by Lieutenant Beirne Lay, Jr.,
then an Army Air Corps pilot and later a Hollywood screen-
writer.

Looking back on the Lindbergh-Earhart era, he wrote, "I
held, at best, a grudging respect for the pilots who performed
spectacular long-distance hops. I was heartily in accord with the
airline slogan, 'There's no more room for heroes in flying.' I
was glad to see aviation being debunked. If Amelia Earhart
flew from Mexico City to Newark Airport, if Wiley Post circled
the globe solo, my attitude, like that of many other fliers, was
something like this: 'Give them credit, sure. They did a good
job. Good navigation. Good pilotage. And good luck. But I
could have done the same thing with the right airplane and
backing. The big hand they get is the result of the public's ig-
norance. It's exaggerated. The ship deserves most of the
credit.' " That was the professional view.*

As for the layman, Lieutenant Lay said, it was apparent that
the public was becoming blasé, and the glamour of extended
flights would "wane in the rising tide of the commonplace
which is overtaking all phases of aviation, with kids learning to
fly and women jostling men for records. . . ."

With Amelia, nothing counted but the flight itself. Nothing
but bad weather or mechanical difficulties would stand in her
way. On March 17, 1937, she and the plane and her crew were
ready for takeoff. The crew on the first hop from Oakland to
Honolulu now included Captain Manning, Fred Noonan, and
an added starter, Paul Mantz, who wanted to visit his fiancée in
Hawaii and who would act as copilot. Rain kept falling until
about 4:30 P.M. The skies then cleared, and the Lockheed Electra was towed out of a Navy hangar.

---

* Lay changed his mind later, he said, after flying a fighter plane from March
Field, California, to Langley Field, Virginia, when he learned how much skill
and endurance were required for distance flights.

Amelia, driven to the head of the 7,000-foot runway in a Navy staff car, took over the controls with Mantz beside her in the cockpit, Manning and Noonan in the cabin behind them.

The Electra roared down the runway and easily lifted its five tons into the air with 4,000 feet of runway to spare. The landing gear was retracted. Amelia took it up to 2,000 feet and then leveled off as they headed over the Golden Gate and out over the Pacific. Their departure had been kept secret, except for a San Francisco *Chronicle* photographer who had been tipped off, had rented a small plane, and got a striking picture of the Electra passing over the Golden Gate Bridge which made front pages all over the country the next morning.

The flight was so smooth, so uneventful, that if any of the participants were superstitious, they would, like actors, have feared the portents of an untroubled dress rehearsal. Just eight minutes short of sixteen hours later they landed at Wheeler Field, near Honolulu.

Along the way Mantz, sharing the cockpit with her, had coached Amelia on reducing her power settings so the Electra cruised at a true airspeed of 150 miles an hour and burned 38 gallons of gasoline an hour. Mantz later told his biographer, Don Dwiggins (*Hollywood Pilot*), that in the past he had "found that Amelia had a tendency to push her engines to the limit, flying with extra power to make up for headwinds. . . . I had to convince her of the danger of this method on critical long-range flights." He also was perturbed because she looked "groggy" at the end of the flight and asked him to land the plane at Wheeler. "I just took a reading on the radio compass— Makapuu Point was dead ahead," Mantz recalled. "I stuck the nose down and started the letdown, through the undercast. It was just about dawn, and we could see the glow of lights. I went around Makapuu Point and then crossed Wheeler Field. I wrapped it around in a steep bank to check the wind sock. AE yelled 'Don't! Don't! She was very fatigued and kind of exuberant. She calmed down when I made a normal approach pattern and we landed. . . ."

His own log of the flight was sketchy and matter-of-fact, and he was amused by Amelia's poetic fancies—almost as though a writer, not a pilot, had been sitting in the driver's seat all the way across the Pacific: "The aft cabin is lighted with a weird green-blue light . . . Our instruments show pink. . . . The sky rose yellow. . . . The sea is lovely. . . . Venus is setting ahead and to the right. . . . The moon is a lifesaver. . . . It gives us a horizon to fly by. . . . It shines on the engine cowls and into the cockpit. . . ."

From Hawaii, after dropping Mantz and refueling, they would make the long leap over the central Pacific to tiny Howland Island, an American possession, where the government had recently built an emergency landing field and the Coast Guard vessel *Itasca* would be standing by to render any necessary assistance.

For the next takeoff, which was dependent on a weather clearance, the Electra was flown over to Luke Field near Pearl Harbor. Amelia wanted to leave almost immediately, after a few hours' rest, but a storm was spotted moving in from the southwest.

The departure was put off until the morning of March 20, which gave Amelia a full day of sunbathing and relaxation at the Waikiki Beach home of Mantz's friends Chris and Mona Holmes. Mantz's fiancée, Terry Minor, was there, too. The Holmeses had arranged a party, complete with luau and hula dancers, but Amelia preferred to walk up the beach by herself. "Amelia was not very social," the next Mrs. Paul Mantz would remember. "She was very nice, but rather hard to know." Many others had noted that friendly but determined aloofness.

Next day everything looked fine for the takeoff, but as she observed, "When things are going very well is just the time to anticipate trouble." Mantz had preceded them to Luke Field to warm up the plane and inspect the fuel, which was commercial gasoline brought over by tank truck. A good thing he did. He found water and sediment in the fuel and hustled up a new supply. Using his charm on the commanding officer of the Hawaiian Air Depot, he managed to buy 590 gallons of the new high-test military aviation fuel.

Amelia, along with Captain Manning and Fred Noonan, climbed into the Electra just as first light was touching the hills to the east of Pearl Harbor.

There were 3,000 feet of concrete runway, with patches of sea visible beyond. As soon as the Electra began trundling down the strip, Amelia knew something was wrong; the plane was sluggish in answering the throttle. It was loaded with 900 gallons of gasoline, more than enough for the flight to Howland, but Amelia had insisted that because of uncertainty about the weather ahead they must have enough fuel to return to Luke after eight flying hours.

Halfway down the runway she knew they were in a May Day situation. The plane wasn't getting up enough speed for liftoff. Suddenly it lurched to the left. The corrective measures Amelia took immediately—throttling back on the left engine—caused the plane to career into a wide circle and then ground-loop. The right landing wheel was sheared off and the right wing badly damaged. Only the sturdiness of Lockheed construction, she said later, prevented a complete wipeout of the ship.

Amelia kept her head even as the plane was going out of control. She cut the switches before it came to a stop and thereby prevented a spark from setting off the gasoline which poured from the ruptured wing tank. None of the plane's occupants was hurt, but it was apparent that the Electra would never fly again unless it was sent back to the mainland for a factory overhaul.

Fire engines raced out to the crippled plane, with Mantz aboard one of them. Amelia had just jumped to the ground, following Manning and Noonan, when Mantz came up. "I don't know what happened, Paul," she told him.

Mantz had warned her against "jockeying" the throttles on takeoff, and he believed that was what had caused the trouble.

"That's all right," he said, putting his arm around her. "So long as nobody was hurt. You just didn't listen to Papa, did you?"

The Electra was dismantled, hauled to the Honolulu docks, and sent back to Burbank for repairs.

Mantz's opinion was that the plane would be airworthy in "a couple of months."

There were differing opinions on what caused the crackup. There was Mantz's that throttle-jockeying was to blame. Some witnesses on the ground said one of the tires blew out, but Amelia studied the tracks on the runway and concluded that this could not have been the primary cause. Some alleged that Amelia had simply lost control of the heavily loaded plane. Others guessed that the extra gasoline had been improperly loaded and had unbalanced the ship. Amelia herself came to no definitive verdict but believed the right shock absorber on the landing gear may have given way.

She refused to give up on the project. Even as the Electra was slithering down the runway with sparks flying and metal crunching, she said later, she thought to herself, "If we don't burn up, I want to try again."

15
The Other Way Around

AROUND-THE-WORLD flight then was a corporate enterprise in itself, calling for a financial structure and an elaborate logistics system. Everything had to be improvised, almost on the scale of a scientific expedition. With the failure at Honolulu, Amelia and her advisers had to recast their plans completely. More money had to be raised for rebuilding parts of the Electra. Gasoline and spare-parts caches had to be rearranged, since it was decided that Amelia would fly west to east on the second attempt; later in the spring the weather patterns, according to meteorologists, made that reversal advisable.

Everything had to be done in a crash program to get the flight started no later than early June; actually, it took off two weeks earlier than that, thanks to a rush job done on the Electra at the Lockheed factory in Burbank.

Even with help from the Odlums and other friends, as Amelia said, she was going to be "more or less mortgaged" far in the future to be able to renew the flight.

Psychologically she was unaffected by the near-disaster on Luke Field. She had always been a fatalist and more than once told her husband and friends that when she died, "I'd like to go in my plane." Putnam, looking back on their life together, would realize that "wholly without melodramatics" she could never visualize herself getting old; death would save her from that indignity. "It *is* hard to be old," she told him once. "I'm afraid I'd hate it."

Because of the delay Captain Manning, on leave of absence from his ship, had to drop out as navigator. Amelia decided that Fred Noonan would share her adventure. Aside from the fact that he could act as copilot as well as navigator, she liked the coolness he had shown when their plane cracked up in Hawaii. When the ground crew wrenched open the cabin door, she learned, they saw Noonan methodically folding up his charts, completely unrattled.

The tall, handsome, blue-eyed Irishman was a veteran of the world of adventure. Chicago-born, he had gone to sea at the age of seventeen and served on the British square-rigger *Compton*. During World War I he had served as an officer on a Royal Navy munitions ship and survived three torpedoings. He stayed in the merchant marine after the war until he became interested in aviation. With his experience as a navigator, he obtained a job with Pan American Airways, learned to fly, and served as both pilot and navigator on the airline's overseas flights. Later he was appointed manager of the Pan Am airport at Port-au-Prince, Haiti, then inspector of all the company's airports. In 1935 he was detailed to map out the line's transpacific routes from San Francisco to Hawaii, Midway, Wake Island, Guam, the Philippines, and Hong Kong. When the first Pan Am China Clipper, a four-engined Martin flying boat, took off on the first Pacific flight, Noonan was aboard as navigator.

Amelia could hardly have found a man with more or better experience as her collaborator, but he had one flaw. It seemed to be the inevitable one in the men to whom Amelia in some measure entrusted her life: alcohol. First her father, then Bill Stultz, now Noonan, who was said to have acquired a two-bottles-a-day habit. He had a better head for the stuff than the senior Earhart or Stultz, and his associates said they never saw him incapacitated for duty because of drinking. Yet Pan Am had let him go as a bad risk.

The association with Amelia Earhart, in fact, constituted Noonan's comeback. He had sworn off the stuff. He was in love with a California girl named Mary Martinelli and married her on March 27, 1937, immediately after returning from the aborted Hawaii takeoff.

Even before they boarded ship for San Francisco, Amelia had more or less decided to take on Noonan as her navigator. She knew about his problem and was a total and understandably dedicated abstainer herself, but there was still enough of the social worker in her to believe in the possibility of rehabilitation.

After telling him Captain Manning would have to go back to his ship, she asked Noonan, "Do you feel up to staying with me?"

Noonan nodded. "I need this flight."

"I mean all the way," Amelia said, "as the only navigator. I've decided against even trying to make part of the flight alone."

"Do you trust me?" Noonan asked.

"I believe in you."

"Then," Noonan said, "I'll give you the best I have."

Putnam was disappointed in her decision to make the whole round-the-world trip with a companion and tried to talk her out of it. The last leg at least, he argued, ought to be flown solo. It would be more dramatic and therefore harvest more publicity, with all the fringe benefits, if she at least landed back in America alone. But Amelia would not be dissuaded; she knew she needed help in handling the big Electra, especially after the Hawaii mishap.

Later (according to Fred Goerner, in *The Search for Amelia Earhart*) Amelia learned that her husband had persuaded Noonan to sign a contract stipulating that he would "stay in the background" as much as possible, even though Noonan had been counting on his fair share of the publicity to help him in starting a navigation school.

Amelia looked embarrassed when she pried the details of that contract out of Noonan, then shook her head and said, "That—unfortunately—is GP. He's an intelligent man, but he can't resist the lust for fame and celebrity. Did you actually sign the contract?"

"Yes."

"Well, I'll solve that problem for you right now," Amelia told him. "GP isn't running this flight. I am, and as far as I'm concerned there's no star billing. We'll share the dangers, and the same goes for the credit."

On May 17, less than two months after the Hawaiian crackup, the Electra had been repaired and rolled out of the Lockheed hangar. From then on, Amelia lost no time in getting the show on the road. On May 18 she tested the plane, and it seemed to be airworthy in every respect. The next day she flew it up to Oakland to pick up Fred Noonan. And on May 20 the round-the-world flight got under way—haltingly. The plan was to fly the Electra to Miami, give it a final tuning up, then cross the thousand miles of Caribbean to Puerto Rico; then to Brazil, Africa, Karachi, Burma, Singapore, Australia, Howland Island, Hawaii, and back to Oakland.

Trouble was still dogging her. She and Noonan, along with George Putnam and mechanic Bo McKneeley, took off in secret from the Oakland airport; the press was not informed that the flight was beginning or even that this time she was going to fly west to east around the world. The plane was carrying a "payload" of airmail covers sold by a New York department store to help pay for the flight, to which Paul Mantz had added a packet for his Hollywood friends Jean Harlow, James Cagney, Clarence Brown, John Ford, Darryl F. Zanuck, Pat O'Brien, Howard Hawks, William S. Wellman, Wallace Beery, Richard

Arlen, Ann Harding, William S. Hart, Ralph Bellamy, Ruth
Chatterton, Robert Montgomery, and Slim Summerville.

All this philatelic baggage almost went up in smoke on the
first leg of the flight. At Tucson, Arizona, they landed for
refueling. Just after the Electra's tanks had been topped off for
the long slant across the United States to Miami, the left engine
backfired and burst into flame.

Amelia cut the switches immediately, but the ground crew
had to extinguish the flames with foam. The damage was slight
enough to be repaired overnight, and they took off again. After
another overnight stop in New Orleans, they arrived in Miami
on May 23.

Paul Mantz was furious when he heard the news that Amelia
had begun the round-the-world venture so suddenly. He was in
St. Louis for an exhibition of aerial stunting and told his partner, Tex Rankin, that he feared she would run into trouble.
He believed that Putnam, whom he disliked, was "pushing her
too hard," making her keep to schedules based not on human
or mechanical requirements but on radio commitments, advertising contracts, lecture tours.

Mantz had urged that before Amelia flew the Electra from
Burbank again there be a final check of its radio equipment
(whose functioning still didn't satisfy him), a rehearsal of the
power settings that would get the most mileage out of the fuel
supply, and more rest and seclusion.

For the next week Amelia and the others waited in Miami
while a corps of Pan Am experts went over the Electra at the
airline's terminal, making final adjustments to the engines and
instruments. One day Amelia was sunning herself on the concrete apron and watching the mechanics work on her plane. Sitting with her was Carl Allen of the New York *Herald Tribune,*
who had been assigned to write the story of the flight from accounts provided along the way by Amelia for the newspaper's
syndicate. Until the flight was under way again, of course, Allen
was sworn to secrecy.

Amelia was in a reflective mood and confided to the newspaperman, "I have a feeling there is just about one more good flight left in my system, and I hope this is it. Anyway, when I have finished this job, I mean to give up the major long-distance flights."

Then, clasping her long, slender hands in her lap, she laughingly added, "I'm getting old and want to make way for the new generation before I get feeble."

She was then a few months short of her thirty-ninth birthday.

Later Carl Allen wrote in the *Herald Tribune* of Amelia's ability to get along with the men working on her plane and how she refrained from showing any impatience when the job of tuning up the Electra took longer than expected. "Being men and being engaged in a highly essential phase of the serious business of air transportation, they all naturally had preconceived notions about a woman pilot bent on a 'stunt' flight —not very favorable notions, either. It was, undoubtedly, something of a shock to discover that the 'gal' with whom they had to deal not only was an exceptionally pleasant and reasonable human being who 'knew her stuff,' but that she knew exactly what she wanted done, and had sense enough to let them alone while they did it. There was an almost audible clatter of chips falling off skeptical masculine shoulders."

The mechanics were also impressed, Allen wrote, by her willingness to help out with the donkey work, if needed, joining them in pushing the plane in or out of the hangar, and by her lack of dismay when her face, hair, or clothing was smeared with grease or oil. "It did not escape the sharp-eyed mechanics that autograph seekers and photographers who hovered about the airport inevitably caught up with the airwoman rather than her catching up with them, and that, while she was unfailingly good-natured and obliging, she ducked these incidents as much as possible."

The men were also pleased when "she ate lunch at the 'greasy spoon' restaurant across the highway from the airport and reported her pleased discovery that the food was as good as that at downtown hotels. She was particularly delighted to find out that the 'greasy spoon' served rich, creamy buttermilk flecked with bits of butter—her favorite beverage."

His former Pan Am associates at first commiserated with Fred Noonan for having to fly with a woman, Allen noted, but "now they were willing to concede that 'poor old Fred' needed no sympathy, that he evidently had signed up with 'the pick of the lot' of women aviators, just as they believed that she chose one of the best aerial navigators in the world." (Noonan himself wrote his bride from Miami that Amelia was "the only woman flyer I would care to make such an expedition with. Because in addition to being a fine companion and pilot, she can take hardship as well as a man—and work like one.")

On June 1 Amelia rose before dawn and drove out to the Miami municipal airport with her husband. Shortly after 5 A.M. she and Noonan took their places in the cockpit; Putnam leaned in from the cabin to say good-bye, as briefly as possible, in accordance with Amelia's aversion to sentimental farewells, and then he and his son David joined the ground crew to watch the takeoff. The departure was conducted with her usual dispatch. At 5:56 A.M. the Electra took wing into the unclouded sky.

That was her farewell, unknowingly, of course, to America. Later she would grin over America's farewell to her in the form of a column written the day of her departure by William Allen White, editor of the Emporia *Gazette,* renowned as the "Sage of Emporia," and a long time ago a classmate of her father's at the University of Kansas. The clipping that caught up with her along the way read: "Amelia Earhart is speeding on her round-the-world flight. She will have long boresome hours with little to do and much to think about.

"If we could catch her we would have just this one message, about as follows: 'Amelia dear, we knew your pappy when he was an amiable, carefree cake-eater in the University of Kansas, fifty years ago. So we have a right to take you aside and tell you something. It is this—we hope to heaven when you were packing your grip you put in a pocket comb. For you certainly need to comb your hair. Now is the time to get the tangles out and give it a good straightening. So in the long lone watches over the gray and melancholy ocean, comb your head, kid, comb your head."

As a matter of fact, she would have had plenty of time for hair-combing in the early stages of her flight if she had been foolish enough to erase that trademarked tousledness.

The Electra was a hundred miles off the Florida coast, heading for San Juan, Puerto Rico, when the Miami radio station WQAM broke into its scheduled programming to report that Amelia Earhart had just taken off safely on the beginning of her round-the-world flight. It pleased her that she had managed to leave without any fuss, any throng at the airport, any swarm of newspaper people. She stayed tuned to the station, by prearrangement, to receive a weather summary prepared by Pan Am meteorologists.

While Amelia piloted, Noonan kept an eye out for islands, lighthouses, reefs, and other features of the seascape below by which they could check their course and speed. By 6:30 A.M. they passed over the Bahama Banks and half an hour later Andros Island, off which they could see a submerged wreck like an undersea shadow.

Amelia locked the ship into the newly installed automatic pilot and jotted some observations: "We look down upon little rocks and reefs which just poke their heads above the water. . . . So few lighthouses in this mess—one pities the poor mariner. . . . On some solider ground we saw trees in black silhouette against the burnished sunpath. . . . A friendly course. Hardly out of sight of one island but another pancakes on the horizon. . . . The shadows of clouds (white clouds in the blue sky) are like giant flowers, dark on the green sea. . . . Curtains of rain clouds aloft . . . the sun shines weakly through the overcast which keeps down temperature; at 4800 feet it is only 80 degrees outside. . . . Sperry [the automatic pilot] has been flying much of the time. . . . Tuned in at about 1300 on a Spanish station and heard my name. . . . Sea and sky are indistinguishable; there is nothing to see. . . . F. N. smells land."

The gyroscopic automatic pilot had made distance flying "pretty sissy," she decided. Noonan was back at the chart table in the cabin and communicated with Amelia by clipping notes to the end of a bamboo pole. At noon, via this rudimentary intercom, he informed her they were slightly off course for San Juan and gave her a new compass heading. They touched down at San Juan about an hour later. For their overnight stay they were guests of Clara Livingston, the island's only woman flier, on her 1,600-acre plantation 20 miles from the capital.

They returned to the airport before dawn the next morning to learn they would have to work out a new route. Amelia had intended to make Paramaribo, Dutch Guiana, on the next hop, but the runway was being repaired; they would have to reduce the weight of the plane and could take only enough gasoline to reach Caripito, Venezuela. There were few airports along the South American coast then, and they had to adjust their plans to the circumstances. The main thing was to make the flight across the South Atlantic, Brazil to West Africa, as short as possible.

Caripito was an oil town in a jungle clearing, but it had a concrete runway and a well-equipped hangar owned jointly by Pan Am and Standard Oil. The following morning, June 3, they took off into dense rain clouds, bucking 148-mile-an-hour headwinds until they picked up the jungle-bordered Surinam River and followed its course to Paramaribo, the capital of Dutch Guiana, then a narrow-gauge railway, a thin scar in the dense growth, to the airport 25 miles outside town.

A Dutch Army unit was drawn up for inspection when they landed and took over the job of guarding their plane overnight. The American consul drove them to the Palace Hotel in Paramaribo. After dinner that night they discussed the fact that heavy rains had made the airport predictably difficult for a takeoff the next morning and wondered if they might be delayed a day or two.

Patience, said Noonan philosophically, was the air or sea mariner's best friend. It was all a matter of comparison. "We're impatient about a day's delay," he said. "That's because that day's lost flying might see us across a continent or an ocean. But a swell way to learn patience is to try a little sailing-ship voyaging. Back in 1919 I was on the bark *Crompton,* then the biggest square-rigged ship under the British flag. We were weatherbound 152 days on the voyage from the state of Washington to Ireland. After nearly half a year on one vessel on one trip you become pretty philosophical about the calendar."

"Yes," Amelia said. "I think I'll stick to airplanes."

The next day they didn't need any philosophy to pull them through. It was clear except for mists over the Surinam, and the Dutch airdrome was dry enough for takeoff. Their next destination was Fortaleza, Brazil, over a course that took them 370 miles over the open sea and 960 miles over Brazilian jungle. If anything went wrong, there was little likelihood of a successful forced landing either in the jungle or on the 180-mile lower delta of the Amazon.

Ten hours later they came down, almost exactly on target with Noonan's estimated time of arrival, at Fortaleza, on a broad sandy plain west of Point Mucuripe. The Pan Am facilities were first-rate, and Amelia decided to have the Electra's engines overhauled and its instruments checked by the airline's mechanics there rather than down the line at Natal, their jump-off for Africa. That meant a two-day layover, part of which Amelia spent shopping for a lightweight raincoat and a sun helmet and part studying the local sociology. "I went tourist," she also confessed, "and took pictures of burros loaded with produce and human beings."

On June 6 they ran down the coast to Natal and its international airport, used by various airlines as the point of departure for flights across the South Atlantic. For several years the French had been running a twice-weekly mail service to West

Africa and had two weather-reporting station ships in the South Atlantic. The French helped with her flight plan and shared their weather information.

The first long ocean hop loomed—1,900 miles to Dakar, then a French colonial city. They took off in darkness at 3:15 A.M. June 7, hoping to make an African landfall before evening.

16

Following the Equator

*T*HE Electra was loaded with 900 gallons of gasoline, and Amelia and her navigator must have thought back to that aborted takeoff from Luke Field, when the plane somehow had balked at its heavy burden. And there were complications on the predawn takeoff from Brazil. The longer runway was lighted, but there was a crosswind blowing. There was a secondary runway which was a shorter, grass-surfaced, and unlighted. They had to survey it, in fact, with flashlights and pick out shadowy landmarks to guide them when the plane lifted off.

Risky as it looked, the takeoff was easy, the Electra functioned perfectly, and soon they were out over the dark sea bucking the prevailing winds. The sky ahead began glowing, and Amelia reflected that this was the third time she had seen dawn over the Atlantic from an airplane.

The weather was much as the Air France meteorologist had predicted. A period of head winds of about 20 miles an hour, then a spell of the doldrums, then clouds would build up with a tropical suddenness and intensity. For a few minutes they rode out the heaviest rain Amelia had ever seen; it pounded so hard she could feel the plane trembling.

During a calm stretch at 6:50 A.M. she scribbled her random impressions: "Just crossing equator, 6000 feet. Sun brilliant. Little lamb clouds below. Ahead dark ones. . . . Ship below. I descend to let him see us for report . . . Doldrums. Rain sends clouds. Sperry flies while I do this. Have just come through very heavy rain. . . . Gas fumes in plane from fueling made me sick again this morning after starting. Stomach getting weak I guess. . . . French and Standard Oil people very careful about wiping oil cans. No ground wire used as in U.S. In refueling at Natal boys spilled so much gas it was funny. I am charged with 165 gals. in a 149 gal. tank. . . . Kinseys sent lunch. Took to field. Odd scene. Frenchmen all rotund. Champagne bottles along walk. Frenchmen waiting their plane from B.A. not in until 6 A.M. . . ."

A flight so calm that she could brood over spilled gasoline and reflect upon the girth of Frenchmen, with the automatic pilot in operation even during the squalls, obviously was a tremendous change from her Atlantic solo of half a dozen years earlier when she had to keep her hand on the stick, strain every nerve and muscle for the whole long flight.

Later on she wrote, "Seven hundred and something to go . . . that's about the mileage between Burbank and Albuquerque. Seems long way off . . . long way too from radio beams and lighted airways . . . our flyers at home don't know how pampered they are. . . ."

The only flaw in the flight was a navigational error, and that was probably due to Amelia's insistence on establishing the fact that, though a female, she was in command. It was a rather dangerous procedure in a way; if you trusted a navigator enough to take him on, and particularly if his experience and skill were greater than your own, you should be bound by his advice.

It happened as they approached the thick haze over the jungled coast of West Africa. Noonan, back at his chart table in the cabin, sent a note via fishing pole to Amelia in the cockpit: They should turn south at 3:36 P.M. for Dakar, their scheduled landing place, which he estimated was 79 miles away.

Amelia shook her head. Instead of a left turn, she believed they should turn north. "What put us north?" she scrawled at the bottom of Noonan's note, indicating she believed he had made a navigational error. Perhaps, too, she was remembering how Captain Manning, on that tryout suggested by Jacqueline Cochran, had missed Los Angeles by about 200 miles.

So she followed her own hunch, rather than Noonan's scientific calculations, and turned north.

Feminine intuition, on that occasion, proved to be a faulty navigational aid. A town with an airfield appeared on the horizon, and Amelia set the Electra down. It turned out to be St.-Louis, Senegal, French West Africa, instead of the larger base of Dakar. Fortunately Air France had fueling and servicing facilities available on the field. "The fault," she admitted, "was mine"—and thereafter she would be less likely to rely on her own hunches.

After an overnight stay in St.-Louis, they hopped up the coast to Dakar for a two-day layover while the plane was checked over and they studied the geography they would encounter on the next log of their flight.

Wandering around colonial Dakar, Amelia thought the streets, thronged with people still dressed in the Mother Hubbard mode introduced by the missionaries, a "tropic comic opera." Then she had a soberer second thought about the contrast between the inherent dignity of the African and the humiliation of the American Negro. "What have we in the United States done to these proud people, so handsome and intelligent in the setting of their own country?"

She and Noonan were guests of the French governor-general, however, and she was persuaded that the French had "a genius for colonization"—a genius somewhat depreciated by events following the world war just two years in the offing. Amelia was delighted with Africa, even its pungent smell, as an echo of her childhood when she and her sister would spend rainy afternoons in the carriage house on Quality Hill and pretend to be African explorers. Reality was even more delightful than the imaginings of childhood. "For me," she said, "the dreams of long ago had come true." She and Noonan spent hours at the governor-general's mansion tracing a route almost due east across the continent. There would have to be an overnight stop at Gao, now part of Mali, which was a trans-Saharan transportation center, and another at Fort-Lamy, Chad, in what was then French Equatorial Africa. A distance of 4,350 miles across the continent would have to be made in four hops.

Shortly after dawn on June 10, equipped with Air France weather charts indicating barometric lows and possible tornadoes in their path, they took off for Gao, 1,140 miles in the interior across Senegalese jungle and then vast stretches of veld and desert. Flying over a desert was more difficult than over an ocean, Noonan wrote his wife, because most of the maps were inaccurate and misleading. "At points," he wrote, "no dependence at all could be placed on them." And there were few recognizable landmarks in the desert. Even so, their navigation was on target. "In all the distance I don't think we wandered off the course for half an hour, although there were times when I wouldn't have bet a nickel on the accuracy of our assumed position."

They landed at ancient Gao, with its seventh-century mosque and lopped-off pyramid, well before nightfall and found the 50-gallon drums of gasoline marked "Amelia Earhart" waiting in a corner of the hangar as had been arranged months before; the logistics system never let them down.

Fortified by a predawn breakfast of mushroom omelet and hot chocolate provided by one of those French chefs who seemed to be the torchbearer of Gallic civilization wherever it had established itself, they departed on the Gao-Fort-Lamy hop over central Africa. "Thousand mile hops" over Africa, she noted, were coming to "seem routine. One quickly becomes accustomed to the feeling that when places are separated by a paltry five hundred miles they may be considered practically neighbors."

So far they had been flying over a gigantic wasteland ruled by the French: mostly desert, *Beau Geste* country, sand-colored forts, occasional mounted patrols of the Foreign Legion. Beneath the brisk and practical exterior Amelia was a confirmed romantic, and she responded accordingly; it all had a beauty of coloring, light and shadow, she believed, "which only the willfully blind could ignore." On the ground it might be a forbidding wilderness, but for the air traveler there were plentiful airports and weather-forecasting services, with a fairly well-traveled airway between Dakar and Khartoum, which was on the Cape-to-Cairo route.

As they sped toward Chad and the midcontinental region, Amelia could not help enthusing over what air transport was doing for Africa. The day of the caravan was fast disappearing. The most remote outposts were being linked by plane services. Even the natives were getting blasé over what they had regarded with wonder a few years earlier. Airplanes were "accepted as being almost as commonplace as camels or tractors." She remembered a cartoon she had clipped and framed for the study of her home in Rye. An African with spear and shield was staring up at a plane in the sky and saying, "Hm, a new Lockheed!"

They flew over the vast shallows of Lake Chad, almost as much swamp as lake, and landed at Fort-Lamy. When they jumped out of the cabin, they saw that the landing gear had buckled. A leak had developed in one of the shock absorbers— the first mechanical trouble they had experienced since leaving Miami a dozen days before. It took the small ground crew at Fort-Lamy until 1:30 P.M. the next day to pump up the shock absorber and fix the leak, so they made a shorter hop than planned to El Fasher in the Anglo-Egyptian Sudan. The atmosphere had turned from French to British and was a little less easygoing. As soon as they landed they were surrounded by a crew of disinfectors, men with Flit-guns who sprayed Amelia and Noonan, their luggage, and the interior of the Electra to destroy any French germs they might have brought with them. Properly disinfected, they were invited to the British provincial governor's house for the overnight stay.

Next day they flew the 500 miles of trackless waste between El Fasher and Khartoum. Amelia locked into the autopilot and amused herself by studying the map for that section of the flight, which had been prepared in California months before, and wishing she could drop down and visit such splendid-sounding places as Qala-en Hahl, Umm Shinayshin, Abu Seid, Idd el Bashir, Fazi, Marabia Abu Fas—though from the air there were no visible villages or oases.

At Khartoum, capital of the Sudan, they landed at an airdrome near the racetrack, waited for two hours while the Electra was being refueled and checked over, and then took off again for Massawa, Eritrea, then an Italian colony. Italians were then undergoing their brief hour of Mussolini imperialism, which had conquered Ethiopia in a war which pitted the spear against the twin-engined bomber, and Amelia couldn't help wondering if she would be graciously received by Il Duce's men. During her Italian visit of several years ago, she had met Italy's leading airman, Air Marshal Italo Balbo, a bearded charmer who had taken her for a frightening ride in his low-slung racing car. After she refused to show the white feather on that ride, they had become good friends, and she hoped he might happen to be in Eritrea.

They flew high over the Eritrean mountains and trusted they would not stray over the nearby Ethiopian border, where unauthorized overflights were likely to be met by a stream of machine-gun bullets from Italian fighter planes. Avoiding that possibility, they landed at Massawa, on the Red Sea, which Amelia was somewhat disappointed to observe was actually blue.

At Massawa they descended into a steam bath, 120 degrees in the shade, and were guests of the Italian commander. There was a language barrier, but they managed to have the engine checked, the oil changed, the tanks refilled. They also refueled themselves when an officer asked if Amelia was hungry and she replied, "As hollow as a bamboo horse," an old childhood saying which her hosts had some difficulty in translating.

Next day they flew the 335 miles to Assab, southeast down the hot barren Eritrean coast. Assab was closer than Massawa to Karachi, at that time part of India, their next destination. It was a long flight over Saudi Arabia and the Arabian Sea, almost 2,000 miles, and they needed the longer runways at Assab to lift their heavily loaded plane. A large supply of gasoline had been stored at Assab. Furthermore, the flight had to be nonstop because the Arabians refused permission to land; at first, in fact, they had even forbidden Amelia to fly over the peninsula but had relented enough to permit an overflight of the southern tip.

Well before daybreak they took off from Assab and followed a carefully plotted course. Not only Arab hostility to the whole venture but the desolation below and the poor chances of surviving a forced landing dictated the most cautious navigation and made that leg of their journey seem the most hazardous thus far. For those back in America who followed the progress of the flight with the most interest and personal concern, the Assab-Karachi hop was an anxious period for another reason. As Amelia learned later by telephone, it had been announced that she was flying direct from Massawa to Karachi, without the stayover at Assab, and her husband, relatives, and friends were worried about her being overdue in India.

The flight took them over the southern entrance to the Red Sea and the southeastern tip of Arabia. They flew over the British protectorate at Aden as a checkpoint, also intending to use it as a landing place if the plane wasn't functioning properly. From Aden they traveled up the southern Arabian coast, keeping a few miles off the mountains and deserts of the Hadhramaut, which looked to Amelia quite as inhospitable as the rulers of that territory. "Some regions," she noted, "looked as if mighty harrows had churned the tortured badlands into a welter of razor-back ridges, fantastic mountains and thirsty valleys barren of vegetation and devoid of life." Poor as their chances would be of surviving a forced landing, they carried a letter in Arabic, composed by two linguists in New York, which would inform any nomadic sheikhs below that they had come in peace and their overflight had been permitted by the king himself.

The Electra bore them swiftly across the Arabian Sea toward Karachi, now the capital of Pakistan, on the Indian coast. Only a minor mechanical disturbance marred the flight: the manual-mixture control lever jammed, and the starboard engine was using too much fuel. Amelia had to reduce their speed in order to conserve fuel.

They landed at the Karachi airport at 7:05 P.M., thirteen hours and ten minutes after leaving Assab. A more formal reception awaited them, but first they were treated to the attentions of another British fumigation squad. Since they had passed through yellow-fever districts in East Africa, they had to be considered possible carriers. There was some talk of a nine-day quarantine, but British Health Service doctors who examined Amelia and Noonan gave them clearance.

There would be a two-day stay in Karachi while the ground crew of Imperial Airways tuned up the Electra and Royal Air Force experts readjusted the instruments. The first familiar face to greet Amelia was that of Jacques de Sibour, who was married to the former Violette Selfridge, heiress to the London department store fortune. De Sibour, a pilot himself, had acted as Amelia's agent in the Orient, arranging for supply caches and obtaining maps and other flight information.

The Maharaja of Jodhpur invited Amelia to fly up to his palace 300 miles cross-country and land at his private airport, but Amelia opted for simpler pleasures during the Karachi stay. The most fun was camel riding. Along with De Sibour, Noonan, and other companions, she visited an oasis several miles outside Karachi on camelback. A camel, she found, was balkier at the controls than an airplane. "I climbed into the saddle swung between his two humps. It was a startling takeoff as we rose. A camel unhinges himself in the most extraordinary fashion. As his hindlegs unfold you are threatened with a nose-dive forward. Then with a lurch that can unhorse (I mean uncamel) the unwary, the animal's center section, so to speak, hoists into the air. It is reminiscent of the first symptoms of a flat spin. Camels should have shock absorbers."

She also had business to take care of during the stopover. The stamp transactions negotiated by her husband helped to pay expenses, so she had to go into the city and have her covers canceled by the Director of Post and Telegraph. Most of her stay, however, was spent watching the ground crew working over the Electra. Some of the longest flights over water were ahead. She wanted to get it all over with; flying had become a grueling job, with little of the poetry and excitement she had experienced years before when she first took up a Kinner Canary.

A woman journalist came out from Karachi, and Amelia willingly submitted to a lengthy interview because the woman was curious about the homelier, more feminine details of long-distance flying. "What a woman pilot wears and what she eats is interesting to other women," the newspaperwoman told her. "But particularly interesting would be a clear picture of the quarters she occupies while flying."

"You mean my cockpit?" Amelia asked.

"Yes, after all that's your workroom. Beyond your home it's the most important room in your life. From its windows you've seen more of the world in a day's flying than most women will see in their lifetimes."

So Amelia gave her a guided tour of the Electra and let her sit in the pilot's seat.

"Since leaving California," the newspaperwoman asked, "how many hours have you actually been in your 'office,' here in the cockpit?"

"Well," Amelia replied, "that's about fifteen thousand miles. At one hundred fifty miles an hour, let's say a hundred hours."

"Which equals," said her interviewer, "about two weeks of working days in a kitchen. And a cockpit is more exciting than a kitchen."

Amelia had to agree with that, and the interview revived her flagging enthusiasm, which may well have been diminished by the oppressive heat of Africa and Asia as well as the long journeys over strange lands and tropical seas.

On June 17 she and Noonan resumed the journey, taking off for Calcutta along a well-established airway 1,390 miles across the subcontinent. They flew over the sandstorms of the Sind desert, then high over mountains from which black eagles sortied. The eagles flew so close to the plane Amelia had "some very bad moments" wondering what would happen if an eagle tangled with a propeller. They passed over Allahabad, knew that the Taj Mahal was close by, but decided not to make any sightseeing detours. Past Allahabad they ran into heavy rain and tricky air currents which swept the plane up a thousand feet while Amelia struggled to keep the nose down.

The outer perimeter of gardens and paddy fields, then the jute mills, and finally the docks of Calcutta appeared on the horizon, and they came down at Dum Dum airdrome. The field was waterlogged, and they sent up a fountain of spray as they taxied toward the hangar. The monsoon was about to break, and that was one good reason not to linger any longer than necessary. "Arriving in mid-June," Amelia said, "we'd been warned the monsoons might fall upon us momentarily. But we hoped to squeeze through before they struck their stride." That ride through the squalls had given them a hint of the bad weather to come.

Amelia and her navigator were driven into the city to spend the night, and she noted in passing through the streets of the Bengal capital that Shirley Temple's film *Captain January* was showing at one of the theaters.

The lowering clouds and oppressive atmosphere which precedes the rainy season in India weighed on her as they dined early and prepared for an early start the next morning. She had diligently read up on the subject of monsoons and knew that from June to September the prevailing wind shifts to the southwest. Their course to Burma was southwesterly. That meant they would be bucking heavy rains and winds "full on our nose."

They were up before dawn the next morning and found Dum Dum drenched from an overnight rain. That meant a precarious takeoff, but the weather experts at the airdrome advised them not to wait for the field to dry off, that more rains were coming and would fall intermittently through the day.

To Amelia it seemed the Electra would never lift off as the plane trundled down the runway and the wet sticky soil clung to its wheels. There was a fringe of trees around the airport which their plane barely cleared with a scraping of the landing gear on the upper branches.

At first the flight to Akyab, Burma, where they planned to refuel before continuing to the Burmese capital of Rangoon for an overnight stop, went fairly smoothly. They passed over the endless rice-paddy country of the Ganges and Brahmaputra mouths, which steamed in the heat and humidity. They came down at Akyab, across the Burmese frontier, and just had time to admire the two gold-leafed pagodas from a distance while the Electra's tanks were being refilled. It was a tiny place in the Burmese jungle, but the airport served as a servicing and refueling stop for KLM, Imperial Airways, and Air France, all of them vigorously competing for the air transport business of southeast Asia. The poet in Amelia was pleased to note that two Imperial four-engined transports parked in the Akyab airport were named Artemis and Arethusa.

Less pleasing were the local weatherman's reports on conditions they would meet on the renewed flight to Rangoon. Wind and rain in storm proportions, he said. Almost as soon as they leveled off after leaving Akyab, they ran into a black wall of storm clouds. Head winds laden with rain battered the Electra. The monsoon rain slanted down so hard, Amelia later observed, that "it beat patches of paint off the leading edge of my plane's wings." They would have drowned in the cockpit, she thought, if it hadn't been watertight. One needed a flying submarine to make it through a monsoon storm.

Visibility was nil in the blinding downpour. The monsoon seemed to wall them in. They tried for two hours to find an opening. First they headed out to sea and flew just above the choppy surface of the Bay of Bengal. Then they turned inland, still looking for a hole in the storm, but they were afraid to fly low because of the danger of ramming into a hilltop. There was nothing left to do but attempt a return, flying blind all the way, to the Akyab airport.

And that was Fred Noonan's job. Amelia's respect for his talents as a navigator had been steadily increasing ever since she had overruled him, mistakenly, on the approach to West Africa. She knew that if she had tried to navigate as well as fly her plane, she would have been lost many times over Africa and Asia. This day, June 18, he was doubly a blessing, literally a lifesaver. "By uncanny powers," she related, "Fred Noonan managed to navigate us back to the [Akyab] airport, without being able to see anything but the waves beneath our plane. His comment was, 'Two hours and six minutes of going nowhere.' For my part, I was glad that our landing gear was retractable, lest it be scraped on trees or waves."

At Akyab the airport people said there probably would not be a break in the monsoon weather for another three months. Amelia and Noonan spent the night in the Burmese town, determined to make up for the delay by flying all the way to Bangkok the next day. But the weather was even worse June 19. This time they went up to 8,000 feet, found the upper air just as thick as that below, and bulled their way through the buffeting winds. After about two hours of that, they decided to come down at Rangoon and call it a day.

Somewhere along the Irrawaddy River they descended into sunlight. There was a broad rice-growing plain below. Somehow they had found a hole in the monsoon. Another 50 miles along the river, dodging through alternate patches of rain and sun, they sighted the golden curlicues of the Shwe Dagon Pagoda in the distance. It gleamed in the sun and served as a beacon.

The American consul not only volunteered his hospitality for the night but provided a car and showed them the sights. Driving down Kipling's "road to Mandalay," Amelia remarked to Noonan that now she knew what Kipling meant by flying fishes in his poem. "That's what aviators are," she said, "when they're silly enough to go up during the monsoons."

The feminist in her was alert to such local curiosities as certain streetcars reserved for the women of sects which forbade them to have any physical contact with men outside of their families—and other women in stalls at the marketplace smoking huge cheroots made of cornhusks rolled around tobacco.

The hop to Bangkok and Singapore the next day was easier than they had expected, though they had to climb through squalls to the 8,000-foot level to traverse the high mountains forming the border between Burma and Thailand. After refueling at the Bangkok airport, they took off immediately for Singapore, eager to make up for lost time, and followed a course across the Gulf of Siam, then down the east coast of the Malay Peninsula. For the first time in days they had clear visibility. On landing at Singapore, they found the American consul-general and his wife waiting to welcome them. "They had the courage to take us for the night," Amelia observed, "even after I explained our disagreeable habit of getting up at three in the morning and falling asleep immediately after dinner."

Their flight the next day, begun before the tropic dawn lit up the skies, took them down the archipelago to Bandung, Java. It was beautiful weather, with beautiful scenery below; coming down into the southern hemisphere they seemed to be entering a gentler world. They could let the autopilot take over and admire the tiny, palm-sprouting islands off the Sumatran and Javanese coasts.

Landing at Bandung up in the densely wooded mountains, they taxied straight into a KLM hangar, where arrangements had been made for a checkout of the engines. Amelia whiled away the time by driving up to the surrounding volcanic peaks, half an hour up the mountain roads from Bandung, and coming across an elderly volcanologist. She was always fascinated by specialists and learned that he was employed by the Dutch government to keep a constant watch on the craters, though there had not been an eruption for almost thirty years. Two dogs accompanying him on his daily inspection of the craters were also rated as government employees; they sniffed the volcanic gases and gave warnings which had saved their master's life several times.

Next day, June 24, they planned to make the long jump to Port Darwin, Australia, but when they appeared at the airport, they found that one of the instruments was malfunctioning. Hours of waiting passed while the technicians tinkered with the long-range navigational instruments. Because it was late in the day when they finally were able to board the plane, they decided to make a shorter hop to Surabaya. En route, Noonan reported that the instruments were still out of whack, so they returned to Bandung. A thorough overhaul was indicated.

Perhaps, it would seem in retrospect, that instrument failure was more ominous than it appeared to Amelia and her navigator.

Not overly concerned, however, they took an excursion to Batavia to visit friends of Noonan's while Dutch Air Force and KLM technicians worked on the adjustments. It wasn't until two days later, June 27, that the plane was pronounced fit for duty. This time they were less ambitious and planned to make an overnight stop at Koepang, on the southern tip of the island of Timor, where they could stay at a government resthouse. It took five hours to reach Koepang, with Noonan reporting the instruments in working order again. Timor is a grassy, windswept island without the lush vegetation of Java or Sumatra. The airport was really only an emergency landing field, without any ground crew or hangars. A stone fence had been built around the field to keep out the wild pigs. Except for a shed where drums of gasoline were stored, there were no buildings in which to shelter the Electra. A horde of natives came out from the village to watch, with considerable amusement, while the two fliers struggled to protect the engines and propellers with canvas covers against the nightly dampness. There was a concert at the resthouse that evening, with one native plinking away on a curious instrument made of bamboo strung with steel and copper wires. They couldn't afford to litter the plane with souvenirs, Amelia said, but "we were sorely tempted to bring one to Bing Crosby for a present."

The most perilous phases of their journey, the long flights over the Pacific, were coming up, and stripping the plane of every ounce of excess baggage was very much on their minds. Crossing the Timor Sea, they landed at Port Darwin, Australia, on June 27 and once again, having left Dutch territory, submitted to the British colonial passion for fumigation. Every time they landed on imperial soil, it seemed, they were greeted with "flit guns," as Amelia called them.

As one means of lightening the plane's burden, they packed their parachutes and sent them back to the States.

"A parachute," Amelia somberly noted, "would not help over the Pacific."

17
Last Days on Land

*T*HE last thoughts of Amelia Earhart, some of them a trifle foreboding, before she and Fred Noonan disappeared into the Pacific skies were contained in the continuing story she was sending back to New York. There it was to be cast into a series of syndicated articles by Carl Allen of the New York *Herald Tribune*. Still later it would be edited by George Putnam and published as a book, *Last Flight,* with its abrupt termination.

Before that final leg of her journey, she was a weary, travel-worn woman, perhaps a lot more exhausted than her last accounts to New York would indicate. She estimated that she and her navigator had traveled about 22,000 miles (in forty days) and had about 7,000 to go. She yearned now for familiar faces and beloved places—home in Rye most of all—and would be glad to close the book on the more adventurous phase of her life. She was determined to be home for the Fourth of July and well in advance of any celebrations of her thirty-ninth birthday. "Whether everything to be done can be done within this time limit," she wrote in her log, "remains to be seen."

It had taken Amelia and Noonan almost eight hours, fighting

head winds all the way, to fly from Port Darwin to Lae, New
Guinea. There had been a two-day stopover at Port Darwin,
unexplained in Amelia's log or the account for the newspaper
syndicate; perhaps both she and Noonan had needed the rest.
Once they reached Lae—the jumpoff for Howland Island, the
second to last scheduled stop before reaching Oakland, California—there would be no time for rest; they would have to take
off the moment weather conditions were favorable.

To reach Lae they had to traverse the Arufa Sea, Torres
Strait, and Gulf of Papua—1,200 miles, mostly over water,
through low-hanging clouds. Menacing though they were in a
sense, the cloud formations were gorgeous. They climbed into
what Amelia called "fairy-story sky country" to clear the New
Guinea mountains. Even at 11,000 feet the sky was "peopled
with grotesque cloud creatures who eyed us with ancient wisdom as we threaded our way through its white shining valleys.
But the mountains of cloud were only dank gray mist when we
barged into them; that was healthier than playing hide and
seek with unknown mountains of terra firma below." Amelia
nosed the Electra down and found that they had negotiated the
peaks successfully and were on the western flanks of the range.
The coastline was below. They flew along the coast until Lae
appeared on the shores of the Huon Gulf.

There were adequate landing and servicing facilities below—
a strip hacked out of the jungle, 3,000 feet long, ending at a
cliff overhanging the waters of the gulf. When they landed, they
even found hangar space for the Electra, though Guinea Airways Company kept the field busy with its operations, flying
passengers and heavy machinery to the goldfields accessible
only by air.

Amelia and her navigator went to a newly built hotel in Lae
after being driven into town past settlements of thatched native
huts built on pilings and hanging out over the water. Late on
the day of their arrival, June 30, they were hopeful of taking off
the next morning for Howland Island. "Tomorrow," Amelia
wrote, "we should be rolling down the runway, bound for

points east. . . . If not, we cannot be home by the Fourth of July as we had hoped, even though we are one day up on the calendar of California. It is Wednesday here, but Tuesday there. On this next hop we cross the 180th Meridian, the international dateline when clocks turn back twenty-four hours."

The next day, July 1, they learned that despite their eagerness to be on their way, they would not be able to take off. The Electra had been loaded to capacity with gasoline and oil for the 2,556-mile jump to the central Pacific. The weather experts, however, advised against a takeoff; the wind was blowing the wrong way and clouds were piling up, and it was felt that they should wait for the most favorable conditions.

Also—and more ominously than Amelia gave any hint in her last transmissions to the United States—Noonan was having instrument troubles. He was "unable, because of radio difficulties, to set his chronometers. Any lack of knowledge of their fastness and slowness would defeat the accuracy of celestial navigation. Howland is such a small spot in the Pacific that every aid to locating it must be available." Noonan knew even better than Amelia how disastrous that might be and worked to calibrate his chronometers with the malfunctioning 50-watt radio set on the Electra. An error of one minute on his chronometers would put the plane four miles off course.

Amelia provided little detail on the efforts made to correct their navigational difficulties. It would almost appear from her writing that other considerations had equal weight. She mentioned the fact that during their two days at Lae they "worked very hard" repacking the plane and throwing out anything not absolutely needed.

They even took time out for sight-seeing, obtaining a truck from the manager of the hotel where they were staying and visiting a nearby native village. Amelia still had enough energy, by her own accounting, to be fascinated by the details of native life, to recall the stories of their New Guinea travels told by her husband's friends Martin and Osa Johnson, who had been among the first to explore the interior of the island. She and

Noonan were amused by the fact that the villagers trained their pigs to act as watchdogs, and "Fred said he would hate to come home late at night and admit being bitten by a pig!" She even bought a dictionary of pidgin English for two shillings. "It was well worth the price to discover that all native women are called Mary. I had some difficulty in understanding why 'to sew' should be 'sew-im-up.' "

The jungle, she discovered, had a "strange fascination" for her. In the last of her writings she indicated that she was afflicted by divergent impulses. "I wish," she said, "we could stay here peacefully for a time and see something of this strange land." But her last written words were: "I shall be glad when we have the hazards of its [the Pacific's] navigation behind us."

Yet there must have been a lot more on her mind than was indicated by Amelia's sketchy account of the two days at Lae—the last two days, probably, of her life. Hitting Howland Island had always been uppermost as the most dangerous part of the venture. In the vastness of the central Pacific it was only a speck. Howland was approximately two miles long by a half-mile wide, with a maximum elevation of twenty feet. It would take dead reckoning indeed, a lot of luck with the navigation, and perfectly functioning equipment to make that landfall. And with the comparatively weak signals which could be broadcast by civilian aircraft radios, they would have to home on those transmitted by the Coast Guard cutter *Itasca,* which had been stationed at Howland for that purpose. Amelia's own account of those last days on Lae, which do not even mention the *Itasca,* is more revealing for its omissions, perhaps, than for what it said.

A cloak-and-daggerish atmosphere long since has enveloped the events preceding her takeoff, but it is clear that the United States government, particularly its armed services, had a strong vested interest in her Pacific flight. In those years the Japanese Empire was rapidly expanding. It had launched a campaign on the Chinese mainland, it had lopped off Manchuria, it was giving birth to the Japanese Co-prosperity Sphere, which encompassed a Japanese hegemony over most of Asia and the western Pacific. On the day Amelia took off for Howland, in fact, the American newspapers were featuring stories about Japanese expansion. Japan had just bluffed the Soviet Union into removing Russian troops from islands in the Amur River, a move which the Soviets hoped would reduce the chances of war along the Siberian frontier and divert Japanese opportunism to other possibilities. That same day James R. Young, Tokyo correspondent for the International News Service, was warning that the Japanese capital "has the feeling of a city that knows war is inevitable." Meanwhile there was a clamor in Congress for the United States to maintain its isolationist stance. As for the belligerency of the Japanese attitude toward the United States, it was amply demonstrated less than six months later when Japanese planes deliberately dive-bombed and sank the American gunboat *Panay* in the Yangtze.

The United States obviously, even in mid-1937, had to be seriously concerned with the possibility of war with Japan. Various military and naval prophets had been warning of the eventuality for forty years, since the surprising Japanese victory over czarist Russia. In any military and naval contest for the Pacific, the United States had been placed at a disadvantage by terms of the World War I peace treaties. Japan had received under mandate of the League of Nations most of Micronesia—the Mariana, Caroline, and Marshall island groups formerly administered by Germany. Japan was forbidden to fortify them or prepare them for any military use but had proceeded to do so, and to keep out all non-Japanese, since the early 1920's. And the Mandated Islands presented a serious threat to American positions, from the Philippines to Hawaii, in the Pacific. Japan now controlled the Pacific islands north of the equator with the exception of Midway, Guam, and Wake.

To counteract the increasing Japanese military and naval strength in Micronesia, particularly in the Marshalls, the United States needed an advance air base on Howland, which would place the more modern bombers within range of the Marshalls and the huge, closely guarded Japanese naval base at Truk. But there was a stumbling block: Howland was under the jurisdiction of the Department of the Interior, and Ernest Gruening, who supervised administration of island territories, decided his budget would not cover the construction of an airfield. President Roosevelt and his military advisers got around that when Amelia, at the urging of Air Corps officers, asked for permission to refuel at Howland instead of Midway, which could be done only if landing facilities were built on Howland. That would have to be done on a crash basis. A Presidential order was issued for the work to be done early in 1937. The Air Corps was delighted because it would have facilities for land-based reconnaissance and bombing planes; furthermore Amelia Earhart's flight, if it was successful, would prove the feasibility of Air Corps operations over the Pacific and encourage the development of long-range aircraft: the Flying Fortresses and Super Fortresses to come. Later, when the time for reflection and recrimination arrived, there were many who believed that the whole round-the-world flight was a military setup; that secret funds had been channeled through Purdue for the purchase of Amelia's new plane; that the concealed purpose of her flight was the construction of a Howland base from which the Japanese forward bases could be pulverized from the air.*

Certainly the United States military had long been obsessed with the strategic strength of the Japanese in that part of the Pacific world. Although not itself a member of the League of Nations, the United States was indignant over Japan's violation of its mandate in fortifying the island groups it had received in custody. As early as 1923 a Marine lieutenant colonel named Pete Ellis, who in 1921 had submitted a report predicting Japan would attack the Hawaiian Islands, was assigned to pene-

---

* Actually the American base on Guam was closer to Truk and the Japanese headquarters on Saipan than Howland Island was. Guam, however, was farther from the Marshalls than Howland.

trate the Carolines and Marshalls. He disguised himself as a German trader. Ellis' mission ended with his mysterious death, which was attributed to poison administered by the Japanese military police.

The Army Air Corps was also deeply concerned by the Mandated Islands, and the leading pioneer of military aviation, General Billy Mitchell, made a tour around the area late in 1923. As a young officer Mitchell had served in the Philippines and absorbed the conviction of most Old Asia Hands that sooner or later Japan would attack United States possessions without warning. His survey of what the Japanese were doing in their protectorate of Micronesia concluded with the prediction that the Japanese would use those islands as forward bases for an attack on Pearl Harbor. Furthermore, with bull's-eye accuracy, he forecast that the surprise attack would be launched on a Sunday morning.

With all their suspicions of what the Japanese were doing in the Marianas, the Carolines, and the Marshalls, United States intelligence officers could prove nothing because Japan refused permission for any foreign ships to enter the Micronesian harbors, and only a few visitors from other countries were allowed to venture there. The League of Nations, weakened by a long sequence of blows to its prestige, was powerless to enforce the provision of the mandate that "no military or naval bases shall be established, or fortifications erected in the territory."

The Carolines, the Marianas, and the Marshalls were closed off; overflights, innocent or otherwise, would be confronted by swarming Zeros, and visitors dropping in from the sky, accidentally or not, would be met with, at best, a cold hostility.

Undoubtedly Amelia had been briefed on most aspects of the western Pacific situation. At least she knew they could not afford to veer very far north of the equator, except over the British-held Gilbert Islands almost due east of Howland. (One odd circumstance was that the British authorities on the Gilberts were not alerted to give her radio assistance.) That last day on Lae she and Fred Noonan must have spent anxious hours over their flight plan. They not only had to find Howland but avoid the Japanese Mandated Islands. If they had any other mission than to make landfall, and there is no absolute proof that they did, that was just one more thing to worry about.

18
Flying into Yesterday

*T*HE last people known to have seen Amelia Earhart and Fred Noonan are those who gathered on the airfield outside Lae to watch their Electra take off, zoom upward from the cliffs overhanging the Huon Gulf, and rapidly become a glint of bright metal on the horizon and then disappear. It was July 2 in Lae, July 1 on Howland. Since the international dateline lay across their flight path, they were flying into yesterday; or put another way, they were gaining a day. Not that it mattered in their case. Their lives were now measured in hours.

They took off with a plane fully loaded with 1,150 gallons of gasoline, enough to carry them 4,000 miles if they didn't run into storms or strong head winds: more than enough to reach Howland even if they had some difficulty with weather or navigation. The island was so small they could not rely on dead reckoning. It was up to Fred Noonan to guide them to their next destination. And that depended to some extent on the weather: It would have to be unclouded for Noonan to take his fixes on the sun by day and the stars by night. Once they were more than 500 miles out they would not be able to stay in radio contact with Lae.

Communication with Lae, as well as the Coast Guard direction finder up ahead, was ruled out by the fact that in Miami Amelia had ordered a 250-foot wire trailing antenna removed; she believed it would be too much trouble to play out and reel in the antenna during a flight. Yet Paul Mantz had insisted on its installation, and his forebodings about the success of the flight had only increased when he heard the news from Miami. Her radio equipment worked well in voice communication, Mantz had been advised by other experts, but it had serious shortcomings as a navigational aid; it wasn't high-powered enough to enable ground stations or ships at sea to take a fix on the plane.

Mantz had gone to the trouble of asking the manufacturer, Western Electric, how to boost the equipment's capabilities. According to Mantz's biographer, Don Dwiggins, a Western Electric executive had wired back: "To obtain satisfactory results on 500 kilocycles, a trailing wire at least 250 feet long should be used."

Mantz did not see how Amelia could home in on Howland Island, on the most perilous leg of her flight, without the trailing antenna he had installed. He was both enraged at the way his expertise had been ignored and fearful for Amelia's safety when Putnam wrote from Miami, blandly overlooking Mantz's advice on the subject, that "between ourselves, the radio gave unending trouble. As I understand it, it was finally decided by the technicians that the longer aerials were improper. One part of them just cancelled out the other, so they shortened the aerials and apparently got the thing pretty well licked. . . ."

According to Amelia's flight plan, the Electra would be within radio range of Howland around daybreak. At Howland the Coast Guard cutter *Itasca* would be waiting to send homing signals (which, of course, Amelia wouldn't be able to receive). On the island itself a new high-frequency direction finder of the most advanced design had been installed as an additional aid. But somehow, apparently because of a lack of coordination between the group on Howland and her own flight headquarters, she had not been informed of the direction finder.

There were two other American ships detailed to offer assistance if necessary. The USS *Swan* was stationed halfway between Howland and Hawaii in case Amelia overshot Howland. The USS *Ontario* was on patrol between Lae and Howland.

The Electra took off at 10:30 A.M. It didn't have too much runway, considering the fact that the 3,000-foot strip hacked out of the New Guinea jungle ended abruptly at cliffs, with the sea far below. It was a struggle getting the heavily loaded plane into the air. But Amelia lifted off with 150 feet of runway to spare.

From then on, all that is known of the flight consists of fragmentary, static-blurred messages, except for the first transmission, which was clear enough. Amelia's call letters were KHAQQ. It was arranged that she would transmit her call signal and any other flight information at a quarter after and a quarter to each hour. The *Itasca* would send homing signals and weather reports on the hour and the half hour.

At 5:20 P.M. (Lae time) the New Guinea station received a message from Amelia giving her position, 795 miles from Lae, on course and not far from the Solomons. No trouble was reported, though she and Noonan were believed to have encountered strong head winds along the way.

On the *Itasca* the long watch had begun. In the communications center Chief Radioman Leo G. Bellarts was standing by at the two receivers and transmitter. Two other men were on duty with the ship's direction finder and the high-frequency model ashore. Also in the radio room on the cutter were Commander W. K. Thompson, the *Itasca's* captain; other officers and enlisted men; Richard B. Black, the field representative of the Interior Department; and correspondents for the Associated Press and United Press.

All through the night these men stood by the loudspeaker in the radio shack straining their ears for Amelia's signals.

The rest of Amelia Earhart's story—the verifiable details—is told in the log of the *Itasca*.

Every hour and half hour its transmitter sent out weather reports and the homing signals. At 12:15 A.M. the *Itasca* sent a message to the cutter *Ontario* asking if it had heard the Electra's signal, but it hadn't. At 1:15 the *Itasca* still hadn't heard from Amelia, but there was no alarm aboard the Coast Guard cutter because it was reckoned that she must be at least a thousand miles off Howland. Ten minutes later the *Itasca* radioed Amelia, advising her that no transmissions had been received from her and requesting that she "please observe schedules with key." There was no answer.

The first fragmentary signal from the Electra came through heavy static at 2:45 A.M. Not much could be learned from that transmission, except for the encouraging fact that they were in contact. The newspaper correspondents listening at the loud-speaker later reported that they could make out Amelia's voice reporting, calmly enough, "Cloudy and overcast," but static drowned out the rest of her words.

On receiving that first message, knowing that maintaining contact might be difficult because of weather conditions, the *Itasca* broadcast to all stations in the Pacific a request that they check whether the cutter's signals were being received. The *Itasca* was heard clearly enough throughout the area. It was Amelia's transmissions that were weak and indistinct.

At 3 A.M. the *Itasca* transmitted the weather report—clear skies, calm seas, ceiling unlimited, east wind at 8 miles per hour —both by voice and key. The cutter then began sending out the homing signal, the letter *A,* which was supposed to bring the Electra through the dawn skies toward a safe landing on Howland.

At 3:30 the *Itasca,* by voice, requested Amelia to give her position and her estimated time of arrival on her next scheduled transmission at 3:45 A.M.

Amelia's voice was heard on schedule: "*Itasca* from Earhart . . . *Itasca* from Earhart. . . . Overcast. . . . Will listen on hour and half hour on 3,105 [kilocycles, her designated frequency] . . . . Will listen on hour and half hour on 3,105. . . ."

The *Itasca* then repeated the request for her position and estimated time of arrival, but there was no reply.

Nothing further was heard from the Electra between 3:45 A.M and 6:15 A.M. At that point Amelia had been airborne for almost eighteen hours; her fuel supply would last about four more hours. She asked for a bearing on 3,105 kilocycles on the hour, would whistle into her microphone so the *Itasca*'s direction finder could get a fix on her position. She added that she was "about two hundred miles out and no landfall."

Half an hour later, at 6:45, Amelia's voice came over the loudspeaker in the *Itasca* radio shack quite clearly and with an unmistakable urgency:

"Please take a bearing on us, and report in half hour. I will make a noise in microphone. About one hundred miles out."

The transmission was too brief, however, for the high-frequency direction finder ashore to get a bearing on her. From then until 7:42 the *Itasca* kept sending her messages asking that she reply on the designated frequency and sending the homing signal.

Then Amelia's voice broke into the tense silence of the *Itasca*'s radio room not at her scheduled time of 7:45 but three minutes earlier. Those who heard it said her voice was high-pitched, edged by alarm:

"We must be on you. But cannot see you. But gas is running low. Been unable to reach you by radio. We are flying at altitude one thousand feet."

That was a rather low altitude for a plane searching for landfall in what, around Howland, was good visibility.

The *Itasca* kept pleading with her to acknowledge its messages, but it was apparent that the radio on the Electra was neither receiving nor sending in reliable fashion.

From Amelia's next transmission at 7:58 A.M. it seemed that she and Noonan believed they had arrived in the Howland area. "We are circling," she advised the cutter, "but cannot hear you. Go ahead on 7,500 [kilocycles] either now or on schedule time of half hour."

The *Itasca* immediately began sending her homing signal without interruption.

From 7:58 to 8:45 nothing more was heard from the Electra, though the *Itasca* urgently radioed Amelia at 8:33, "Will you please come in and answer on 3,105. We are transmitting constantly on 7,500 kilocycles. We do not hear you on 3,105. Please answer on 3,105. Go ahead."

By then the tension in the radio room of the *Itasca* was almost unbearable. The Electra's radio equipment obviously was malfunctioning, and if Amelia couldn't lock in on the *Itasca's* homing signals, it would take sheer luck to bring her in safely. Noonan, it would seem, had been unable to continue celestial navigation because of the "cloudy and overcast" conditions Amelia had reported during the night. And the plane's gasoline supply would last only another hour or so. There was no way of knowing whether Amelia, at last report, was really only 200 miles off Howland, as she believed.

The 8:45 transmission from the Electra was anything but reassuring. Amelia's voice was strained with anxiety as she reported: "We are on a line of position 157 [degrees] -337 [degrees]. Will repeat this message on 6,210 kilocycles. Wait, listening on 6,210 kilocycles. We are running north and south."

To this the *Itasca* immediately replied: "We heard you OK on 3,105 kilocycles. Please stay on 3,105. Do not hear you on 6,210. Maintain QSO on 3,105."

The *Itasca* kept urging Amelia to reply on her assigned frequency.

For the next hour, until 10 A.M., the *Itasca's* radio mast continued crackling with urgent pleas to Amelia to come in on her frequency, to give her position, to maintain contact as best she could.

But the loudspeaker amplifying any transmissions from the plane was silent. It stayed silent as the hands of the clock passed

10 A.M.—the time when it had to be presumed the Electra would be running out of fuel, though Amelia might have more flying time, possibly until noon, if she rigorously conserved her gasoline.

At 10 A.M. a feeling of doom began to settle on the men crowded into the *Itasca*'s radio shack. There was a glimmering of hope, but no more, that if Amelia was circling north of Howland, she might be able to land on one of the British-protected Gilbert Islands.

19
"Find Amelia Earhart"

W*ITHIN* fifteen minutes of the time when it was presumed Amelia Earhart's plane was exhausting its fuel supply, the largest sea search in the history of the U.S. Navy was begun, and it gathered force and numbers in the next several days. The *Itasca* led off at 10:15 A.M. July 2 (Howland time) by steaming at flank speed toward the northwest. Commander Thompson had to make a quick decision on where to begin his sweep of thousands of square miles of ocean and had slender evidence on which to base it. Amelia's only position report had been "We are on a line of position 157-337," but no reference point was given. The *Itasca*'s only hope was to start searching in the northwest quadrant indicated by the 337-degree reference. If she had wandered slightly off course to the south in her attempt to obtain a sighting of Howland, she could have landed at Baker Island, 38 miles south of Howland.

The *Itasca* continued transmitting to the Electra even as she steamed northwest at top speed. There was a possibility that even if the Electra was down, she could be kept afloat for a while and Noonan might get the radio in better working order. There was also a possibility she might have ditched just off one of the Gilberts, in which case she might not be heard from for days. There was even a possibility, not a pleasant one, that she might have had to land at or near one of the Japanese-held Marshall or Caroline islands.

Later that day the Navy dispatched a long-distance reconnaissance plane from Pearl Harbor piloted by Commander Warren W. Harvey to join the search in the Howland area. The next morning the commandant of the 14th Naval District, with headquarters at Pearl Harbor, forwarded a message from Commander Harvey to Commander Thompson on the *Itasca*: "About 420 miles north of Howland. Last two hours in extremely bad weather between altitude 2,000 feet and 12,000 feet. Snow sleet rain electrical storms. In daylight conditions look equally bad. Cloud tops appear to be 18,000 feet or more. Am returning to Pearl Harbor. Now have 900 gallons of fuel on board."

It was probable that Amelia's plane had run into the same violent and widespread storm. With clouds extending up to the 18,000-foot level, she would have been unable to fly high enough for Fred Noonan to shoot star sights and obtain a fix on their position.

In Washington President Roosevelt ordered the Navy to use all available men and ships and planes to join in the search as soon as possible. Aside from the fact that the President and Mrs. Roosevelt were personal friends of Amelia and her husband, Roosevelt must have felt a degree of personal responsibility for whatever might have happened to Amelia. The designation of Howland as her first stop in the central Pacific, instead of Midway, had been engineered by executive order, which directed the construction of landing facilities on Howland. The Navy Department immediately forwarded the order of the Chief of Naval Operations, Admiral William D. Leahy, for a search of the 250,000 square miles of central Pacific by an aircraft carrier, a battleship, four destroyers, and a minesweeper.

The night of July 3 the carrier *Lexington* was docked at Santa Barbara, California, preparing for a Fourth of July reception for civilians. Instead, it weighed anchor and headed out to sea, to be joined en route by three destroyers, the *Drayton,* the *Lamson,* and the *Cushing.*

The *Lexington* contingent did not reach the search area until July 13, upon which, shortly after dawn, it launched sixty planes to hunt for Amelia and Noonan west and east of Howland Island. In the next five days the carrier's planes searched an area of 151,000 square miles.

The *Lexington* task force conducted an intensive search of a 120-mile radius around Howland and including the Gilbert Islands. In a subsequent report of his actions—all of which had negative results as far as turning up the missing Electra or its occupants—Captain Leigh Noyes of the *Lexington* came to certain conclusions which he summarized as follows:

The information actually available indicated that the plane arrived in the vicinity of Howland Island at about eight o'clock in the morning of 2 July. During the night run the navigator should have been able to check his position accurately and frequently by star sights, and it must be assumed that this was done, and that the navigator knew the position of his plane and the ground speed it had been making through the night. [This, of course, did not take into account the storm reported by Commander Harvey on his search by seaplane out of Pearl Harbor or Amelia's own report that they were flying through overcast skies.] Information available on the weather conditions do not indicate that any radical change in direction or force of the wind occurred at Howland Island during the two and one-half hours preceding eight o'clock.

At 0615 the plane reported that they were 200 miles out; one hour and forty-five minutes later they circled and attempted to pick up the island. This time agrees very well with the time it would take the plane to cover 200 miles at 111 knots, and it also checked with the time at which the *Itasca* reported hearing the plane's radio at its greatest strength. All of the above indicates that the plane's 0615 position was reasonably accurate.

This being the case, it is not reasonable to suppose that the plane was more than sixty miles off its course one hour and forty-five minutes later. Having arrived at the navigator's position of the island the plane maneuvered to make a landfall, circling first, and then running north and south indicating they were fairly sure of their longitude. With the gasoline supply practically exhausted . . . it is not likely the plane ventured more than forty miles from the navigator's best position. Assuming that the gasoline gave out when the plane was at the end of one of these runs farthest from the island, the distance from Howland would be only 100 miles.

Captain Noyes' report raised one most significant point— that Amelia's transmissions came through loud and clear twice in the several hours before silence fell, indicating she was quite close to Howland, as she believed.

While the air and sea search was being pressed, the Lockheed engineers who were responsible for the design and construction of the Electra were sought out and interviewed on the possibility that Amelia and her navigator might survive a forced landing at sea. The Electra's empty tanks would keep her afloat, they estimated, for nine hours at the most. But her radio could not operate with the plane on the sea because it was powered by the right engine.

The battleship *Colorado* and the minesweeper *Swan,* the latter having been on patrol between Howland and Hawaii while the flight was in progress, joined the search on July 7, searching south and east of the Phoenix Islands, then north and west of the Gilberts. The *Colorado* had been on a cruise to the Hawaiian Islands, and Dr. M. L. Brittain, the president of the Georgia Institute of Technology, along with the presidents of Northwestern University and the universities of California and

Colorado, had been among the civilian guests aboard the battle-ship. Six years later (in an interview with the San Francisco *Chronicle,* April 13, 1943) Dr. Brittain recalled: "When the *Colorado* reached Hawaii we had a radiogram from President Roosevelt telling us to proceed toward Howland Island to search for the famous American woman flier because we were some 2,500 miles closer than the *Lexington,* the carrier which later joined the search. We discussed the Japanese Mandated Islands and the rumors that the U.S. government had sent person after person to take a look-see, trying to discover whether or not the Japs were illegally fortifying their possessions [sic]. We got a very definite feeling that Amelia Earhart had some sort of understanding with officials of the government that the last part of her flight around the world would be over those Japanese islands."

Even while the search was getting under way, the most sinister and persistent rumor regarding Amelia's disappearance, and the possible cause of it, was going into circulation. Even a scholar of Dr. Brittain's eminence was not immune to it; he relied on a "feeling" that she was on a secret mission to spy on Japanese military and naval activity.

George Putnam had been waiting in San Francisco to greet Amelia when she landed at the Oakland airport and completed her round-the-world flight. His last talk with her had been over the shortwave radio from Karachi, when he was still in New York. Their last exchange, recorded by a dictaphone in the New York *Herald Tribune* office, had been Putnam's query, "Is everything about the ship okay now?"

"Yes," Amelia had replied.

"Good night, hon."

"Good night. I'll be sitting in Oakland waiting for you."

Putnam was stunned by the news flash that Amelia was missing and shocked by succeeding bulletins that she might not survive a forced landing at sea. He always had as much confidence in Amelia's ability to fly through anything as she had in herself —perhaps more, because she understood more completely the chanciness of every phase of her calling.

His first action was to send a radiogram to the naval search headquarters at Pearl Harbor: "If they are down, they can stay afloat indefinitely. Their empty tanks will give them buoyancy. Besides, they have all the emergency equipment they'll need— everything." By everything, he meant a life raft and some emergency rations.

Even with his confidence in Amelia's survival quotient, he knew that they would have to be rescued quickly, perhaps in a matter of hours, especially if she or Noonan had been injured in a rough landing, certainly within days.

His anxiety increased hourly, and in his desperation he remembered Jacqueline Cochran's claim to extrasensory powers which he had dismissed somewhat tartly, to her annoyance. If ESP could locate Amelia, he was willing to become a believer. As Miss Cochran recalled, "George Putnam was in my apartment in Los Angeles almost as soon as he could get there after the news of her nonarrival at Howland Island. He was extremely excited and called on me for the kind of help Amelia thought I might be able to give.

"I told him where Amelia had gone down; that with the ditching of the plane Mr. Noonan, the navigator, had fractured his skull against the bulkhead in the navigator's compartment and was unconscious; but that Amelia was alive and the plane was floating in a certain area. I named a boat called the *Itasca* which I had never heard of at the time, as a boat that was nearby, and I also named another Japanese fishing vessel in that area, the name of which I now forget. I begged Putnam to keep my name out of it all but to get ships and planes out to the designated area. Navy planes and ships in abundance combed that area but found no trace. I followed the course of her drifting for two days. It was always in the area being well combed. On the third day, I went to the Cathedral and lit candles for Amelia's soul, which I then knew had taken off on its own long flight. I was frustrated and emotionally overcome."

And she concluded, "If my strange ability was worth anything it should have saved Amelia. Only the urging of Floyd [her husband] ever prompted me to try my hand at this sort of thing again. . . ."

The more orthodox search went on day after day, with naval vessels and carrier planes crisscrossing the waters of the central Pacific (but taking care not to stray into Japanese air space or coastal areas in the Mandated Islands) and smaller ships calling at every island and combing every coral reef for some evidence of what had happened to the Electra and its occupants. Two privately owned vessels were chartered to cruise as far south as Gardner Island and the Phoenix Islands, British possessions, north to Christmas and Fanning islands, and then to the west.

What they were looking for now, two weeks after the plane presumably had gone down, was the wreckage of the Electra; the possibility that Amelia and her companion could have survived on some tiny island or on their life raft was dim indeed. There was also some hope that they either had landed on one of the Japanese islands or had been picked up by one of the ubiquitous Japanese fishing vessels that plied those waters, but it never materialized. The Japanese said they knew nothing of the termination of Amelia's flight.*

There was great pressure on the Navy, of course, to come up with some answer to the riddle of the Electra's disappearance. The press and public, both in the States and around the world, clamored for a solution to the mystery.

The Coast Guard cutter *Itasca*, while combing the Gilberts, sent an officer ashore at Tarawa, the British administrative headquarters, to confer with the British Resident, who ex-

---

* George Putnam requested the Japanese consulate in San Francisco to relay his plea that all Japanese fishing boats, tramp steamers, and shipping of all kinds keep a lookout. There was no response to his request.

pressed surprise that the two radio stations in those islands had not been informed of Amelia's flight and asked to help in its navigation. Neither of the stations had picked up her messages, fragmentary as they were, while she was approaching Howland. Yet her course lay only 20 miles south of the southernmost of the Gilberts.

A widespread and intense radio watch was maintained throughout the search period in the faint hope that if the missing fliers had reached some deserted island or coral reef they might be able to send a signal.

Ham operators, some of them with vivid imaginations, joined unbidden in the watch. Back in the States both professional and amateur operators kept reporting they had picked up SOS signals from Amelia. On being checked out, such reports indicated wishful thinking or a desire for notoriety. No such signals were heard by the Navy and Coast Guard operators with their more powerful equipment.

The Federal Communications Commission had to issue a warning that it was against the law to report false radio messages. But the public hysteria only mounted as the days passed and the headlines grew bigger and blacker. One of the first false upsurges of hope was raised by a *March of Time* radio broadcast which reenacted the Earhart disappearance and caused the same sort of commotion that resulted from Orson Welles' dramatization of a fictional Martian invasion, which sent thousands of listeners fleeing to the hills. The impressive voice of Westbrook Van Voorhis, the program's announcer, was mistaken for that of an official spokesman at the White House or Navy Department. This broadcast, misinterpreted each step of the way through official channels, resulted in orders dispatched from Pearl Harbor to the searching ships and planes to run down the false tip.

Sometimes the viciousness of rumor was almost incredible, particularly when false hopes were deliberately raised. On July 4 naval radio operators picked up a message, quite garbled, which read: "281 North Howland call KHAQQ beyond north don't hold with us much longer above water shut off." The next day the *Itasca*, the *Swan*, and the British steamer *Moorsby*, after an identical message was heard by an Oakland ham operator, swung out of their search pattern to investigate the indicated position 281 miles north of Howland. High hopes were felt aboard the *Itasca*, whose captain radioed Secretary of the Treasury Henry Morgenthau, Jr.—the Coast Guard being under the jurisdiction of the Treasury Department—"For Secretary Morgenthau: Intercepts of ragged transmissions indicate possibility Earhart plane still afloat 281 miles north Howland. Bearings radio direction finder on Howland confirm approximate position. We will arrive indicated position this afternoon about 1700 plus eleven and one-half time." A short time later a commercial radio station in Honolulu intercepted another dispatch: "*Itasca* sighted flares and proceeding toward them."

Across the nation the morning newspapers jumped the gun, reported in boxcar type: EARHART FOUND!

Twice the men aboard the Coast Guard cutter saw what appeared to be greenish flares to the northeast, and the *Itasca* steamed full speed in that direction. . . .

Back in Los Angeles, Paul Mantz punctured that false hope by advising the newspapers that there were no flares aboard the Electra, that Amelia had forgotten them and left them in the Burbank hangar. It turned out that the flares the *Itasca* crew thought it saw were a shower of meteors.

Mantz himself believed that Amelia and her navigator had "one chance in a thousand" of having survived a crash landing at sea. Two things could have happened to them, he told reporters. "One: The navigator missed the island and Miss Earhart flew until out of gas, and due to fatigue tried to land too high over the clear water which would result in the ship 'falling off,' causing a crash that would kill them instantly. Two: If the sea were very rough, it would be quite hard to judge the distance properly, thus causing her to fly into a heavy roller, having a similar result."

By late in July the whole area, with the Japanese-controlled areas excepted, had been searched, and not one sure clue to the disappearance had been found. The failure was dramatically symbolized for the American people when the *Lexington*, its fuel and other supplies exhausted by a fifteen-day effort, steamed through the Golden Gate. As the carrier plowed into San Francisco Bay it lowered its colors to half-mast in tribute to the lost fliers.

Lost—but not forgotten.

Already the speculation, much of it necessarily ill-informed, had begun and would intensify.

The public was not satisfied to be left with a mystery. It seemed an indignity, somehow, that the life of Amelia Earhart, then undoubtedly the most heroic and inspiring figure of American womanhood, should be closed in such a manner. Where no ending of indubitable authenticity could be supplied for her life, no suitable conclusion for her legend arrived at, the public imagination would take over. Amelia Earhart, once a living woman, had become a part of American mythology.

20
No End to the Mystery

ALMOST inevitably the death of a famous or notorious person arouses a whirlwind of speculation. The ordinary fact of death is somehow unacceptable. The rumor factory works on a round-the-clock schedule. Various investigators, largely self-nominated, rush into print with their theories and find an eager audience.

When a legend as well as a person dies, the human intellect craves to discover a significance that cannot be supported by the facts. With an almost superstitious intensity, a large sector of the public will guess at what it cannot know. It becomes prey to rumors and guesses; it feverishly casts aside facts and logic. People delight in simplifying, in manufacturing a black-and-white explanation for themselves without any gray shades of qualification. The oldest of the communications media, antedating Gutenberg, is word of mouth; it is probably also the most effective. People are always more likely to believe what another person tells them rather than the disembodied pronouncements made through the official channels. There is always the suspicion that the "big shots" are holding something back.

One has only to recall the warped versions that circulated regarding recent events that have assumed a mythic character. Although President Kennedy was killed in full public view, a large section of the public refuses to accept the findings of the Warren Commission; some even believe that Kennedy is still alive and leading a vegetablelike existence in a well-guarded hospital. Just after New York City's Great Blackout of 1965, there was a wave of rumors that it had been caused by sabotage, others that it was an unannounced air-raid test by the government. A number of people believe that Adolf Hitler is alive and well in Argentina, forensic proof to the contrary. For several weeks in 1969 it was firmly believed that Paul McCartney of the Beatles was dead for various illogical reasons, and it took a full-scale publicity campaign to prove the contrary. Somehow the public imagination balks at straightforward, uncomplicated explanations as somehow not befitting the legendary stature of the celebrated dead. After the assassination of Abraham Lincoln, a lush growth of rumor sprang up, even including a theory that he had been killed on orders of his Secretary of War. The death of President Harding, just before the Teapot Dome scandal broke, was made the occasion of reports that he had been poisoned or that he had committed suicide.

In the case of Amelia Earhart, the speculation was greatly enhanced by the close-mouthed attitude of the federal bureaucracy, a seeming reluctance by the Navy, in particular, to be entirely frank about what it learned, and the State Department's traditionally guarded approach to anything that might cause friction with another nation, even a recent enemy.

The favorite theory—and it has not been diminished by the years—is that Amelia Earhart and Fred Noonan were captured by the Japanese, probably because they had secretly undertaken a mission from naval intelligence to spy on Japanese fortification of their Mandated Islands, and that subsequently they were executed. To those who like an admixture of melodrama with their history, that seems to be a satisfactory explanation of what happened to them. It supplies a heroic ending, much more glamorous than the possibility that their plane simply ran out of gasoline and went into the drink.

Yet those most intimately connected with Amelia Earhart, those most familiar with her career, were unanimously inclined to reject such solutions to what others regarded as a mystery. "To produce a sensational denouement for Amelia's story," as her sister, Muriel, has written, "recent biographers have mingled hearsay and possibility and have irresponsibly called it probability." As far as her family was concerned, "the manner of Amelia's death is not of great moment. . . . That she did not live to have a child of her own and enjoy the honors she earned is sad."

Amelia's contemporaries in the pioneering of aviation, familiar as they were with the hazards she faced in that time of uncertain navigational aids and rudimentary radio transmissions, concluded that she simply lost out in the greatest gamble of her life. "For months and years," wrote Ruth Nichols in *Wings for Life,* "her friends and family clung to the forlorn hope that somewhere, somehow, she might still be alive, that once again they would see that cropped golden head and that boyish grin, hear that gay voice and grasp that strong, slender hand. But after almost twenty years have passed, I feel now as I did then—that Amelia flew on across the trackless Pacific until her last drop of fuel was gone and then sank quickly and cleanly into the deep blue sea." It was enough for her that Amelia would "live on in memory as young, golden and unafraid." Jacqueline Cochran also, with or without ESP, was satisfied that Amelia had died at sea. Captain Eddie Rickenbacker on a World War II mission crashed in that area of the Pacific and with his crew was rescued from their raft only after an ordeal of twenty-four days. He had time for considerable reflection on Amelia's fate. "There has always been a persistent rumor that she fell into the hands of the Japanese," he wrote in his autobiography, "but I have always doubted it."

The milling of rumors and the manufacture of hoaxes began almost from the moment that the U.S. Navy gave up its search and pronounced Amelia and Noonan missing and presumed dead.

George Putnam was the victim, eager as he was to find any shred of hope that his wife was still alive, of one of the earliest attempts to profit from her disappearance. A former seaman had conceived a plot to extort money from Putnam. He had found one of Amelia's scarfs in a hangar at Wheeler Field, Hawaii, while she was preparing for her first, abortive attempt to fly around the world from east to west. Using that scarf as proof that he knew what had happened to Amelia, he approached Putnam with an offer to tell her husband which islet in the Carolines her plane had crashed into. She was being held prisoner by smugglers. The man, who demanded $5,000 for his information, was questioned by Richard Black, the Department of Interior representative who had awaited Amelia's landing on Howland; he was trapped by his lies and forced to admit that he had concocted the story. Putnam refused to press charges, saying, "I know Amelia would not want it that way."

Putnam also considered himself victimized by a Hollywood film company's fictionalized version of what happened to his wife. The film, *Flight for Freedom*, with Rosalind Russell hardly typecast in the Earhart role, told of a famous woman flier whom the U.S. Navy asked to fake a disappearance on a flight over the South Pacific; using the search for her as a pretext, the Navy's reconnaissance planes were enabled to photograph Japanese island fortifications. In the film, the navigator was her former fiancé. Putnam didn't much like that, he announced, and filed suit against the producers, which was settled out of court.

The film, produced during World War II, naturally increased the speculation that Amelia had been captured by the now much-hated Japanese. It was embroidered by theories that she had been personally requested by President Roosevelt to fly over the Japanese Mandated Islands and observe what she could of Japanese militarization of the islands.

Yet her sister was unable to find any written trace of such a request in either Amelia's papers or those in the Roosevelt library at Hyde Park, New York. Mrs. Roosevelt told Muriel Earhart Morrissey that her husband had never spoken to her about a mission to spy on the Japanese. Mrs. Morrissey has expressed her own conviction that President Roosevelt "would not have expected Amelia to make the large-scale detour necessary to fly over any Japanese territory."

The recurring efforts to "prove" what happened to her sister meet with little encouragement from Mrs. Morrissey. A retired schoolteacher who lives with her husband on a hilltop at West Medford, Massachusetts—not far from the Amelia Earhart Mystic River Dam and Basin—she believes in looking forward and spends three days a week teaching English to Spanish-speaking women in the Roxbury ghetto. Much like her sister in appearance and personality, in her forthright manner Mrs. Morrissey deprecates the sensationalism of recurrent attempts to solve the mystery but admittedly is puzzled by the air of secrecy maintained by the government.

One sober-minded effort in that direction that impressed her was that of a Michigan schoolteacher, Ann Pellegrino, who several years ago found a Lockheed Electra and reconditioned it. A pilot in her spare time, the intrepid Mrs. Pellegrino decided to duplicate Amelia's last flight in every possible way. She followed Amelia's route at approximately the same time of year. The striking feature of that mission—as she revealed to Mrs. Morrissey at the termination of the flight in Newton, Kansas—was that she encountered impenetrable fog off Howland Island, and without the modern navigational equipment available to her, she might also have missed that tiny dot in the Pacific herself; the duplication was too close for comfort.

This suggested the cloak-and-daggerish explanations of Amelia's fate are out of sync with probability. Obviously the flight from Lae to Howland was more than hazardous enough without the long swing to the north that would have been necessary to pass over any of the Japanese-occupied islands.

Amelia's plane was not equipped with any high-altitude photographic equipment, which alone could have made such an overflight worthwhile from the intelligence viewpoint. The only camera aboard the plane was an ordinary Kodak Duo 620, the type any tourist might carry.

There are other arguments against casting Amelia in the role of aerial espionage agent. She was a pacifist, for one thing; she abhorred anything to do with militarism. Neither she nor Noonan had any experience, training, or indoctrination to qualify them for observing, mapping, or drawing sketches of military or naval installations. And how much could they have been expected to glimpse on a high-speed, high-altitude flight, likely to be interrupted at any moment by Japanese fighter planes or antiaircraft fire—and in the middle of the night at that?

George Putnam remarried eighteen months after Amelia's disappearance but continued to run down every report concerning her that seemed worth checking. He served as a major in the Air Force during World War II and was stationed in the China-Burma-India theater. A variety of false leads was checked out by Putnam as American forces began pushing across the Pacific. There were even claims that Amelia was Tokyo Rose, that she had been captured, brainwashed, and forced to broadcast anti-American propaganda over the Japanese radio.

After the Japanese surrender Jacqueline Cochran, who headed the WASP's, an organization of women ferry pilots, during the war, went to Tokyo on a mission for the Air Force. Although she was supposed to be investigating the activities of Japanese women in their country's war effort, she took time out to dig into the archives at Imperial Air Force headquarters in hopes of finding some clue to Amelia's fate. She did find an Earhart file—as well as others on herself, Jimmy Doolittle, and other celebrated American pilots—but it consisted of newspaper clippings and photographs; there were no documents indicating that Amelia had fallen into Japanese hands.

Just before the war, in June, 1940, Paul Mantz received a letter from Captain Irving Johnson of the yacht *Yankee,* which had just been cruising through the Gilberts. If his information was correct, Amelia and Noonan had been navigating accurately but had simply lucked out. Captain Johnson had just talked to a missionary on the island of Beru. "They have a radio there and when Miss Earhart was lost, he attempted to find out from the thousands of natives in the London Missionary Society's control whether any airplane had been seen at the time. He said that, in certain cases, it was hard to tell whether some ignorant native had actually seen an airplane or wished he had, but that *it was believed that the Earhart plane had flown eastward high up over the island of Tabiteuea.* He said that not a particle of a wrecked plane or of any wreckage that could possibly be from a plane had been found on any of the islands, although the natives often walk along the reefs to see what they can pick up in the way of drift. . . ."

During and after the war a whole crop of Amelia Earhart reports and rumors was harvested and painstakingly winnowed by American officers.

When the Marshalls and the Marianas were captured in 1944, the American forces were ordered in a Pentagon directive to keep an eye out for any evidence concerning Amelia, particularly on Saipan, which had been Japanese headquarters for that area. The search was spurred by a Marine Corps unit's discovery of an album of pictures detailing Amelia's flying career. Saipanese and Japanese prisoners of war were interrogated but could supply no worthwhile leads. (For the Electra to have crashed on or near Saipan, of course, would have required highly erratic navigation—not utterly impossible considering the rough weather Amelia and Noonan encountered—and would have meant they were 2,600 miles off course. But in that case how could the *Itasca* have received messages from Amelia the strength and clarity of which indicated she was not far from Howland?)

After the war ended, the Navy Department, confronted by so many rumors that it *knew* what had happened to Amelia, officially declared that the disappearance was still a mystery;

that she had not been on a mission for any branch of the United States government; that it had no evidence that she had been a prisoner of the Japanese or had been killed by them.

But there was still life in the Earhart legend, and it still made good copy for the newspapers. One flurry of interest had been stirred when a coast artilleryman stationed on an island off Alaska found a piece of driftwood with a message inscribed on it reading, "To my husband—I have crashed 250 miles from Hawaii—N.W. Our motors went into flames—sharks about me. A.E." Another hoax.

Among the more convincing stories told in the wake of the American conquests in the Pacific was that of a Saipan native, Josephine Blanco, later Mrs. Maximo Akiyama and a California resident. She was working for an American dentist on her native island in 1946 and told him of recalling that two Americans had crashed in their plane in 1937 when she was eleven years old. She told of seeing the pair, one a woman with cropped hair wearing a man's clothes, the other a tall man, brought ashore and marched away by Japanese soldiers. They were marched up the road toward the Japanese barracks, shots were heard, and the Americans were not seen again.

The most determined efforts to learn exactly what had happened to Amelia Earhart and Fred Noonan were launched in the early Sixties by Fred Goerner, a Columbia Broadcasting System newsman and broadcaster in San Francisco and author of the fascinating chronicle of his search for evidence, *The Search for Amelia Earhart*. Mr. Goerner, largely financed by CBS, roved the Pacific islands and tracked down every possible clue to the disappearance in a major feat of journalistic enterprise.

Some of the evidence he turned up did not survive closer inquiry. The generator of a civilian-type plane sunk in Saipan harbor was dredged up and brought back to the United States. Paul Mantz, who was to lose his life while stunting a plane for a Hollywood film several years later, agreed the generator was the same type as had been installed in the Electra; he had worked on its engines himself. An expert employed by Bendix, the generator manufacturer, examined it and found that the serial number indicated it had been manufactured in Japan. On another expedition to Saipan Mr. Goerner found a shallow grave in a Saipan cemetery which he believed might contain the remains of Amelia Earhart and Fred Noonan. The bones were shipped back to the United States, attended by much publicity, late in 1961. An anthropologist engaged by CBS, however, reported that the bones were those of three or four different persons, none of them Caucasian.

All this is not to downgrade Mr. Goerner's efforts or decry his purpose; he should have been garlanded with Pulitzer Prizes. Certainly, as the leading unofficial expert on the mystery, his conclusions warrant a sober consideration. In his book he points to the previously unpublicized fact that military-type Wasp Senior engines capable of a top speed of 220 mph were installed on the Electra and believes their purpose was to allow Amelia to make a side trip over the Japanese fleet base at Truk. He believes that she did make that dangerous overflight without being spotted by the Japanese, that she flew on toward Howland, got lost, ditched her plane off what she thought was one of the British-held Gilberts but turned out to be Mili Atoll in the southeastern Marshalls, was captured along with Noonan, and was eventually killed by the Japanese on Saipan.

There were several intriguing facets exposed by Mr. Goerner's investigation. One was the evasiveness of military, naval, and civilian bureaucrats in Washington whenever he tried to find documentary evidence to support his findings and the eagerness to stamp "top secret" on documents which might reveal bureaucratic incompetence. Certainly it would appear that the government, whatever the degree of responsibility it had for seeing to the safety and success of Amelia's flight over the Pacific, eager as it had been for her to make the Howland stop, had not protected her as well as it might. Another fascinating angle was that the late Fleet Admiral Chester W. Nimitz, who had been commander-in-chief in the Pacific theater during

World War II, and who must have read any relevant documents concerning the Earhart flight and its consequences, strongly encouraged Mr. Goerner's investigation and did everything he could, in retirement, to forward it. In concluding his book, Mr. Goerner asked for a Congressional investigation to penetrate any remaining official secrecy, demand answers to the questions he raised, and finally determine what happened to Amelia Earhart and Fred Noonan. It has not been done, though more than four years have passed.

So the story of her life ends with a probably insoluble mystery, an unsatisfactory conclusion to one of the most remarkable American lives. The manner of her death, as her family and friends insisted, is no longer of paramount importance. The real tragedy, as newspaper columnist Jay Franklin wrote at the time, was that "the very qualities which brought her fame in the late 1920's are no longer needed by the late 1930's. A single decade has brought such changes in aviation that chance and guesswork have been largely eliminated. The future lies with the undramatic experts who bring the planes in on time, safely. The romantic whoopla artists have outstayed their aeronautical welcome, and the individual once more becomes submerged in the organization."

It was also noted at the time of her death that she disappeared just when Pan American and Imperial Airways were establishing a routine round-the-world air service. "One plane missing," as a newspaper editorial on her disappearance remarked, "far out on the lonely Pacific. Another plane heading into the dawn, half a world away. And the day of the ocean pioneers is closed."

Amelia Earhart herself recognized that her last flight closed an era and unavailingly hoped to go into a graceful retirement. It was her thirty-nine years, not the moment of her death, that counted. Those years are a continuing inspiration to all who believe in humanity's ability to surpass itself, to reach for the stars.

Aerial Records Set
by Amelia Earhart

Aerial Records Set by Amelia Earhart

June, 17, 1928—First woman to fly across the Atlantic as a passenger.

April 8, 1931—Altitude record for autogiros, 18,451 feet.

May 20–21, 1932—First woman to fly solo across the Atlantic.

August 24–25, 1932—Women's nonstop transcontinental speed record, Los Angeles to Newark, 19 hours, 5 minutes.

July 7–8, 1933—Broke her own transcontinental speed record, Los Angeles to Newark, 17 hours, 7 minutes.

January 11–12, 1935—First to solo from Honolulu to mainland (Oakland).

April 19–20—First to solo from Los Angeles to Mexico City.

May 8, 1935—First to solo from Mexico City to Newark.

June–July, 1937—First to fly around the world at the equator (not completed).

A Note on Sources and Bibliography

*A*MELIA EARHART told much of her own story, particularly the aerial phases, in *The Fun of It, Last Flight* (edited by her husband), and *20 Hrs., 40 Min.* Other sidelights on her career are provided by such flying colleagues as Ruth Nichols, Jacqueline Cochran, and Louise Thaden, all of whom were sympathetic friends as well as occasional competitors. By far the most insight into Amelia Earhart as a person, during all stages of her career, is provided by her sister, Mrs. Muriel Earhart Morrissey, in her memoir *Courage Is the Price.* Her husband, George Palmer Putnam, was also informative and candid on many phases of her career in his biography, *Soaring Wings,* and autobiography, *Wide Margins.* The files of the late New York *Herald Tribune* are most helpful in tracing her last flight, since that newspaper's syndicate published her accounts along the way. Many of her flight logs and other papers have been collected by the library of Purdue University.

The author is indebted to Mrs. Morrissey, in person and in her own writing on the subject, for invaluable help in understanding her remarkable sister. In her own way, Mrs. Morrissey is quite as remarkable and impressive. The term sibling rivalry could not have been invented for the Earhart sisters. I am also grateful for the assistance of the staff of the Manuscript Division and other departments of the Library of Congress and of Lisa Kruse of the Boston Athenaeum's excellent library. Diane Dorsey of the Amelia Earhart collection in the Schlesinger Library at Radcliffe College was also most helpful. The library has a sizable collection of Earhart photographs, family records, and other memorabilia.

The principal published sources for this book were:

Balchen, Bernt, *Come North with Me*. New York, 1958.

Briand, Paul L., Jr., *Daughter of the Sky*. New York, 1960.

Byrd, Richard E., *Skyward*. New York, 1928.

Cochran, Jacqueline, *The Stars at Noon*. Boston, 1954.

Davis, Kenneth S., *The Hero*. New York, 1959.

De la Croiz, Robert, *They Flew the Atlantic*. New York, 1959.

Dwiggins, Don, *Hollywood Pilot*. New York, 1967.

Earhart, Amelia, *Last Flight* (edited by George Palmer Putnam). New York, 1937.

———— *The Fun of It*. New York, 1932.

———— *20 Hrs., 40 Min*. New York, 1928.

Ford, Corey, *Coconut Oil*. New York, 1931.

Goerner, Fred, *The Search for Amelia Earhart*. New York, 1966.

Howe, Ed, *The Story of a Country Town*. New York, 1928.

Jenkinson, Sir Anthony, *America Comes My Way*. New York, 1941.

Lindbergh, Charles A., *The Spirit of St. Louis*. New York, 1953.

Morrissey, Muriel Earhart, *Courage Is the Price*. Wichita, 1963.

Nichols, Ruth, *Wings for Life*. Philadelphia, 1958.

Putnam, George Palmer, *Soaring Wings*. New York, 1939.

———— *Wide Margins*. New York, 1942.

Railey, Hilton H., *Touch'd with Madness*. New York, 1938.

Rickenbacker, Eddie, *Rickenbacker*. New York, 1967.

Thaden, Louise, *High, Wide and Frightened*. New York, 1938.

Index